my **revisi⊙n** notes

AQA AS/A-level Year 1

BIOL

Mike Boyle

HODDER
EDUCATION
AN HACHETTE UK COMPANY

Hachette UK's policy is to use papers that are natural, renewable and recyclable products and made from wood grown in sustainable forests. The logging and manufacturing processes are expected to conform to the environmental regulations of the country of origin.

Orders: please contact Bookpoint Ltd, 130 Milton Park, Abingdon, Oxon OX14 4SB.
Telephone: (44) 01235 827720. Fax: (44) 01235 400454. Email education@bookpoint.co.uk

Lines are open from 9 a.m. to 5 p.m., Monday to Saturday, with a 24-hour message answering service. You can also order through our website: www.hoddereducation.co.uk

ISBN: 978 1 4718 4201 6

© Mike Boyle 2015

First published in 2015 by

Hodder Education,
An Hachette UK Company
Carmelite House
50 Victoria Embankment
London EC4Y 0DZ
www.hoddereducation.co.uk

Impression number   10 9 8 7 6 5 4 3 2 1
Year   2019 2018 2017 2016 2015

Cover photo reproduced by permission of Sebastian Duda/Fotolia

Typeset by Integra Software Services Pvt. Ltd, Pondicherry, India

Printed in Spain

A catalogue record for this title is available from the British Library.

Get the most from this book

Everyone has to decide his or her own revision strategy, but it is essential to review your work, learn it and test your understanding. These Revision Notes will help you to do that in a planned way, topic by topic. Use this book as the cornerstone of your revision and don't hesitate to write in it — personalise your notes and check your progress by ticking off each section as you revise.

You can also keep track of your revision by ticking off each topic heading in the book. You may find it helpful to add your own notes as you work through each topic.

Tick to track your progress

Use the revision planner on pages 4 and 5 to plan your revision, topic by topic. Tick each box when you have:

- revised and understood a topic
- tested yourself
- practised the exam questions and gone online to check your answers and complete the quick quizzes

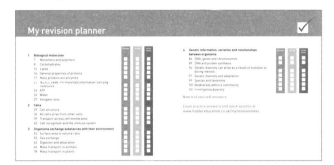

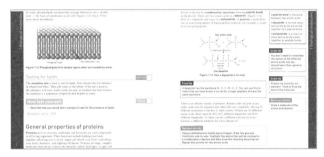

Features to help you succeed

Exam tips

Expert tips are given throughout the book to help you polish your exam technique in order to maximise your chances in the exam.

Typical mistakes

The author identifies the typical mistakes candidates make and explains how you can avoid them.

Now test yourself

These short, knowledge-based questions provide the first step in testing your learning. Answers are at the back of the book.

Definitions and key words

Clear, concise definitions of essential key terms are provided where they first appear.

Key words from the specification are highlighted in bold throughout the book.

Revision activities

These activities will help you to understand each topic in an interactive way.

Exam practice

Practice exam questions are provided for each topic. Use them to consolidate your revision and practise your exam skills.

Summaries

The summaries provide a quick-check bullet list for each topic.

Online

Go online to check your answers to the exam questions and try out the extra quick quizzes at **www.hoddereducation.co.uk/myrevisionnotes**

My revision planner

REVISED   TESTED   EXAM READY

Exam practice answers and quick quizzes at www.hoddereducation.co.uk/myrevisionnotes

Now test yourself answers

Exam practice answers and quick quizzes at
www.hoddereducation.co.uk/myrevisionnotes

Countdown to my exams

6–8 weeks to go

- Start by looking at the specification — make sure you know exactly what material you need to revise and the style of the examination. Use the revision planner on pages 4 and 5 to familiarise yourself with the topics.
- Organise your notes, making sure you have covered everything on the specification. The revision planner will help you to group your notes into topics.
- Work out a realistic revision plan that will allow you time for relaxation. Set aside days and times for all the subjects that you need to study, and stick to your timetable.
- Set yourself sensible targets. Break your revision down into focused sessions of around 40 minutes, divided by breaks. These Revision Notes organise the basic facts into short, memorable sections to make revising easier.

REVISED ☐

2–6 weeks to go

- Read through the relevant sections of this book and refer to the exam tips, exam summaries, typical mistakes and key terms. Tick off the topics as you feel confident about them. Highlight those topics you find difficult and look at them again in detail.
- Test your understanding of each topic by working through the 'Now test yourself' questions in the book. Look up the answers at the back of the book.
- Make a note of any problem areas as you revise, and ask your teacher to go over these in class.
- Look at past papers. They are one of the best ways to revise and practise your exam skills. Write or prepare planned answers to the exam practice questions provided in this book. Check your answers online and try out the extra quick quizzes at **www.therevisionbutton.co.uk/ myrevisionnotes**
- Use the revision activities to try out different revision methods. For example, you can make notes using mind maps, spider diagrams or flash cards.
- Track your progress using the revision planner and give yourself a reward when you have achieved your target.

REVISED ☐

One week to go

- Try to fit in at least one more timed practice of an entire past paper and seek feedback from your teacher, comparing your work closely with the mark scheme.
- Check the revision planner to make sure you haven't missed out any topics. Brush up on any areas of difficulty by talking them over with a friend or getting help from your teacher.
- Attend any revision classes put on by your teacher. Remember, he or she is an expert at preparing people for examinations.

REVISED ☐

The day before the examination

- Flick through these Revision Notes for useful reminders, for example the exam tips, exam summaries, typical mistakes and key terms.
- Check the time and place of your examination.
- Make sure you have everything you need — extra pens and pencils, tissues, a watch, bottled water, sweets.
- Allow some time to relax and have an early night to ensure you are fresh and alert for the examinations.

REVISED ☐

My exams

AS Biology Paper 1

Date:..

Time:..

Location:..

AS Biology Paper 2

Date:..

Time:..

Location:..

1 Biological molecules

Monomers and polymers

The biochemical basis of life

All living things are made from just four basic types of **organic compound**: proteins, carbohydrates, nucleic acids and lipids.

These organic compounds perform similar functions in all organisms. For example, all organisms have DNA as their genetic material and all use it to make proteins according to the same code. The chemical reactions that occur inside cells are controlled by proteins called enzymes. The similarities and differences in these molecules provide clear evidence for evolution.

Some of these molecules are **polymers** — large molecules made from many repeated subunits called **monomers** joined in a chain. Monomers relate to polymers as follows:

- **Amino acids** join to make proteins.
- The **monosaccharide** glucose joins to make the polysaccharides starch, cellulose and glycogen.
- **Nucleotides** join to make the nucleic acids DNA and RNA.

Lipids, on the other hand, are not polymers.

> An **organic compound** is one in which the molecules are based on carbon, i.e. proteins, carbohydrates, nucleic acids and lipids.
>
> A **polymer** is a long chain of repeated units. The individual units are called monomers.
>
> A **monomer** is one of the small similar molecules that join together to form a polymer. There are three important biological monomers: amino acids, monosaccharides and nucleotides.

Hydrolysis and condensation

Think of these reactions as 'breaking down' and 'building up again'. Large molecules are broken down into smaller ones by **hydrolysis**. Small molecules are built up into larger ones by **condensation**.

The food we eat contains a lot of polymers. Digestion involves breaking down these large molecules so that they are simple, soluble and can be absorbed into the blood (Figure 1.1). Large molecules are hydrolysed by enzymes to produce smaller molecules. Once inside the body, smaller molecules are built up into large ones by condensation. For example, we might hydrolyse the protein in a piece of chicken into amino acids that can be absorbed into the body. These amino acids could be used to build up the proteins the body needs such as **haemoglobin**, enzymes and muscle protein.

> A **hydrolysis** reaction breaks a chemical bond between two molecules and involves the use of a water molecule.
>
> A **condensation** reaction joins two molecules together with the formation of a chemical bond and involves the elimination of a molecule of water.
>
> **Haemoglobin** is the red pigment that transports oxygen.

ABCDEFG**H** → A + B + C + D + E + F + G + H → GFEADBCH

Large molecule   Hydrolysis   Smaller molecules   Condensation   Large molecule

Figure 1.1 Digestion involves hydrolysis and condensation

Exam tip

Condensation and hydrolysis are common themes for exam questions. Make sure you get them the right way round. Condensation reactions *produce* water, whereas hydrolysis reactions *use* water. These reactions are the exact opposite of each other.

Now test yourself

TESTED

1 What type of reaction will join monomers to form polymers?
2 Which type of reaction will break polymers down into monomers?

Answers on p. 108

Carbohydrates

Monosaccharides and disaccharides

REVISED

Carbohydrates contain just three elements: carbon, hydrogen and oxygen. Simple carbohydrates are called sugars, which are all sweet, soluble compounds whose names end in *–ose*. There are two types of sugar: **monosaccharides** (single sugars) and **disaccharides** (double sugars).

The three monosaccharides you need to know are glucose, galactose and fructose. The three disaccharides you need to know are maltose, sucrose and lactose.

> **Exam tip**
>
> Try not to get confused with G words. Glycogen is a polysaccharide. Glucose and galactose are monosaccharides (simple sugars).

Glucose

Glucose is a vital molecule and you need to be able to draw its structure (Figure 1.2). The other two monosaccharides, **galactose** and **fructose**, are isomers of glucose — they have the same atoms but in a slightly different arrangement.

Glucose is our main energy source: our cells respire glucose most of the time. This means that the energy in the glucose is released and used to make ATP. In turn, ATP can provide instant energy for activities such as the contraction of muscles (see p. 24).

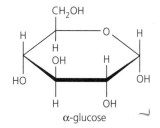

Figure 1.2 The structure of a glucose molecule

α-glucose and β-glucose

Glucose has two **isomers**, α-glucose and β-glucose (Figure 1.3). There is a slight but important difference between these molecules. α-glucose polymerises to form the energy storage compounds starch and glycogen, whereas β-glucose polymerises into cellulose, a compound with completely different properties.

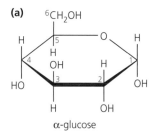 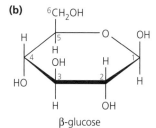

Figure 1.3 Comparing molecules of (a) α-glucose and (b) β-glucose. Note that the carbon atoms are numbered clockwise from the oxygen

A **condensation reaction** between two α-glucose molecules forms a **glycosidic bond** that produces **maltose** (Figure 1.4). Starch is formed by simply repeating the process.

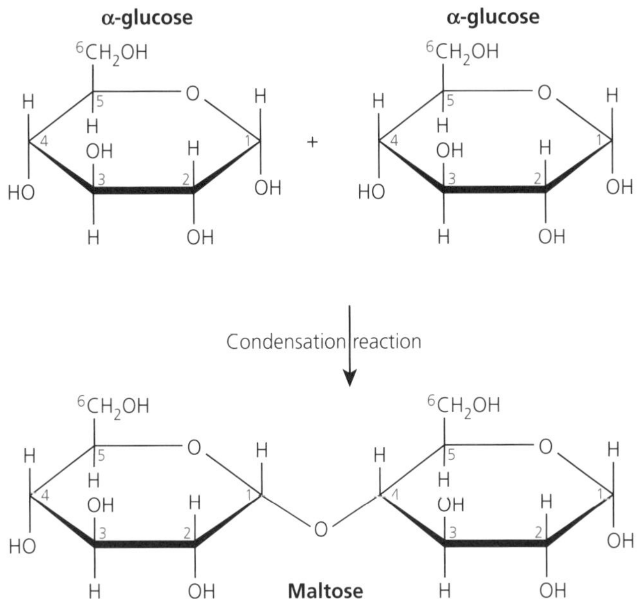

α-glucose   α-glucose

Condensation reaction

Maltose

Figure 1.4 Two α-glucose molecules join to form a molecule of the disaccharide maltose. The bond formed is called a glycosidic bond and it is based around a shared oxygen atom

Sucrose and lactose

These two other disaccharides are made from different monosaccharides:
- one molecule of **sucrose** (cane sugar) is formed by the condensation of one α-glucose molecule and one fructose molecule
- one molecule of **lactose** (milk sugar) is formed by the condensation of one α-glucose molecule and one galactose molecule

Typical mistake

When drawing OH groups, the oxygen is always attached to the carbon and the hydrogen is always attached on the outside of the oxygen. So, when drawing molecules it should always be –OH or HO–, not –HO or OH–.

Polysaccharides   REVISED

Polysaccharides are also called complex carbohydrates. The three polysaccharides you need to know are starch, glycogen and cellulose. These are large molecules made from hundreds or thousands of glucose molecules joined together. Their large size makes them insoluble.

Starch

Starch is the main energy storage compound in plants. Plants make glucose by photosynthesis and then convert it into starch for storage, so it does not take up too much space and does not make the water potential of the cytoplasm too low. Starch is not one compound but a mixture of two: amylose and amylopectin (Figure 1.5):
- **Amylose** is a straight chain polymer of glucose, which means that it is one long spiral molecule with just two ends — there is no branching.
- **Amylopectin**, in contrast, is branched so that there are many more ends. This is important because new glucose units can only be added or released from the ends. Amylopectin can therefore be built up and broken down much more quickly than amylose.

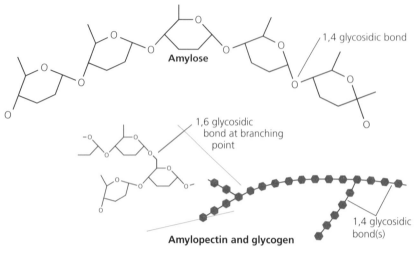

1,4 glycosidic bond

Amylose

1,6 glycosidic bond at branching point

1,4 glycosidic bond(s)

Amylopectin and glycogen

Figure 1.5 The structure of amylose and amylopectin

A storage compound needs to be compact, insoluble and available when needed. Starch does this role perfectly because:
- the spiral shape of amylose makes it compact
- its huge size makes it insoluble
- the branching of amylopectin provides lots of ends that can release glucose quickly

Glycogen

Learning about **glycogen** is easy: it has the same structure as amylopectin, but it is more frequently branched. As a result, it can be broken down and built up more quickly, which matches the greater energy needs of animals.
- Most of our glycogen is stored in the liver and muscles.
- When blood glucose levels are low, glycogen is broken down to restore levels.
- Think of glycogen as short-term energy storage, whereas lipids are long term.

Cellulose

Cellulose is the most common polysaccharide in the world. After water, it accounts for a large percentage of the weight of most plants, including trees. It is a key component of wood.

Starch and glycogen are polymers of α-glucose, whereas cellulose is a polymer of β-glucose. Cellulose has one key property: it forms fibres that have great strength. β-glucose molecules join together in the same way as α-glucose: by condensation reactions that form glycosidic bonds. The difference is that β-glucose units condense to form long, straight unbranched chains. When they lie alongside each other, in parallel, many hydrogen bonds form along the whole length, so that long, strong fibres form. Many microfibrils become glued together by a mixture of shorter glucose chains to form a tough wall that resists expansion (Figure 1.6).

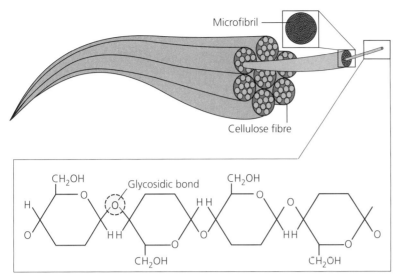

Figure 1.6 In cellulose, chains of β-glucose molecules lie parallel to form strong microfibrils

Now test yourself

TESTED

3 Explain how the structure of cellulose is related to its function.

Answer on p. 108

Testing for reducing and non-reducing sugars

REVISED

Benedict's solution is used to test for the presence of **reducing sugars** (e.g. glucose). It can also be used, indirectly, to test for **non-reducing sugars** (e.g. sucrose). For reducing sugars, dissolve the test substance in water, add Benedict's reagent and heat to almost boiling point. In a positive result, an orange precipitate forms. If it is negative, it stays blue. For non-reducing sugars, a Benedict's test will be negative. So, add a few drops of dilute hydrochloric acid and boil. Then neutralise the solution by adding a few drops of dilute sodium hydroxide. Finally, add Benedict's reagent and reheat again. If positive, a precipitate forms and the solution changes colour from blue to orange. This happens because the non-reducing sugar has been split into its constituent reducing sugars.

The Benedict's test can also be quantitative — it can be used to determine *how much* reducing sugar is present. There are several ways of doing this, in increasing order of accuracy:
1 Assessing the depth of colour by eye (it goes from vaguely greenish to deep orange).
2 Assessing the depth of colour using a colorimeter.
3 By filtering, drying and weighing the orange precipitate (which is copper oxide).

Now test yourself

TESTED

4 What is the difference between a qualitative test and a quantitative test?

Answer on p. 108

Testing for starch

Testing for the presence of starch is simple — add a few drops of **iodine solution**. In a positive result, the sample changes colour from yellowish brown to deep blue/black.

Lipids

Lipids are what most people think of as fats and oils. The two vital properties of lipids are:
● they do not mix with water
● they store a lot of energy compared with an equivalent amount of carbohydrate or protein

The two types of lipid you need to know about are triglycerides and phospholipids. Overall, triglycerides store energy, whereas phospholipids make plasma membranes.

Triglycerides

Triglycerides are formed by the **condensation** of one molecule of **glycerol** attached to three molecules of **fatty acid** (Figure 1.7). Triglycerides are the main energy storage compounds in animals. They contain the elements carbon, hydrogen and oxygen.

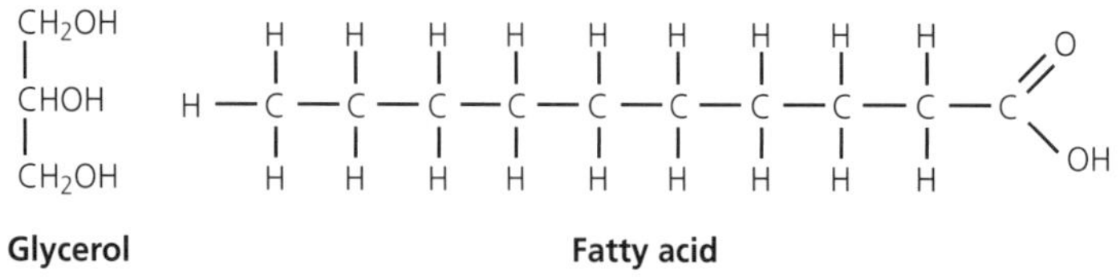

Figure 1.7 The basic structure of glycerol and a fatty acid

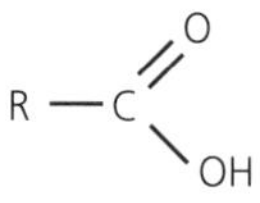

Fatty acids are also called organic acids or carboxylic acids (Figure 1.8). They all have a −COOH group attached to a carbon chain. The carbon chain is known as the R group, giving fatty acids the general formula RCOOH. Glycerol is always the same, but different fatty acids produce different triglycerides (Figure 1.9).

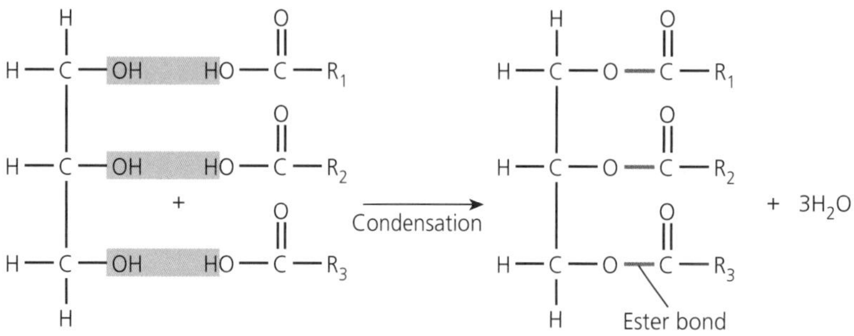

Figure 1.8 The generalised structure of a fatty acid. The hydrocarbon chain is just replaced by an R

Figure 1.9 A triglyceride molecule consists of four subunits: one glycerol joins by condensation to three fatty acids. The new bonds are called ester bonds

Fatty acids

The R group of fatty acids can vary in two ways:
● the number of carbon atoms in the chain
● the number of $C = C$ bonds in the chain

If there are no C=C bonds, the fatty acid is said to be **saturated** because it has as much hydrogen as possible. If there is one C=C bond, there must be two fewer C–H bonds and the fatty acid is said to be **unsaturated**. If there are two or more C=C bonds, the fatty acid is **polyunsaturated** (Figure 1.10).

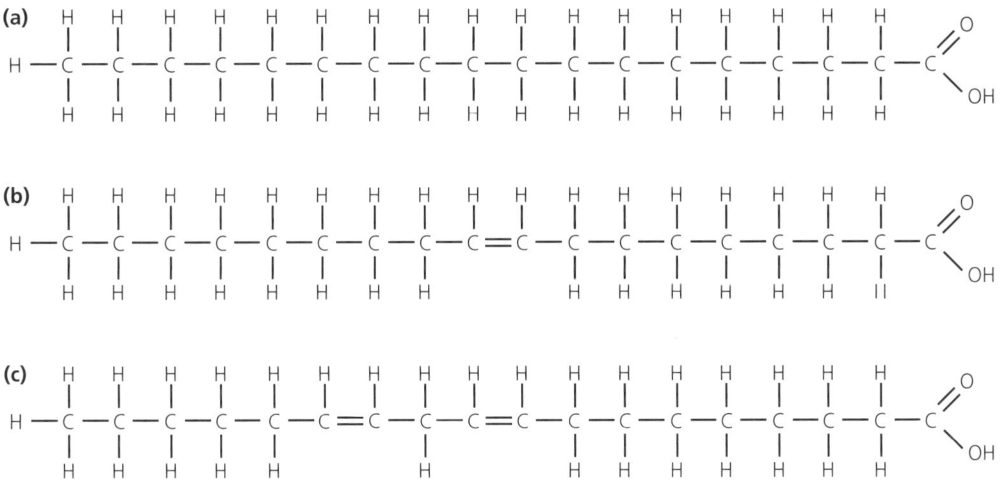

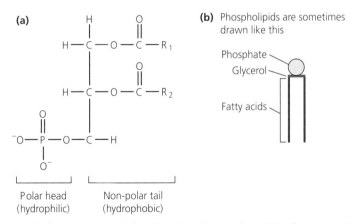

Figure 1.10 Fatty acids: (a) saturated, (b) unsaturated and (c) polyunsaturated

Typical mistake

Candidates often make the mistake of stating that saturated fats have no double bonds. However, they do have a C=O bond, just no C=C bonds.

Fatty acids in animal triglycerides tend to be saturated and solid at room temperature (for example, lard). Plant fats tend to be unsaturated and are usually oils at room temperature.

Phospholipids

REVISED

Phospholipids differ from triglycerides in that they contain a **phosphate-containing group** (PO_4^-) instead of one of the fatty acid molecules. Phospholipids therefore contain the elements carbon, hydrogen, oxygen and phosphorus.

The phosphate-containing group is vital. Instead of the whole molecule repelling water, the phosphate group attracts water. The result is that you get a molecule with two ends: a phosphate group that attracts water and two fatty acid tails that repel water (Figure 1.11).

Figure 1.11 (a) A phospholipid. The head is hydrophilic (attracted to water) and the tails are hydrophobic (repelled by water). (b) A simplified phospholipid

In water, phospholipids automatically arrange themselves into a double layer — the basis of membranes in all cells (Figure 1.12). See p. 39 for more about membranes.

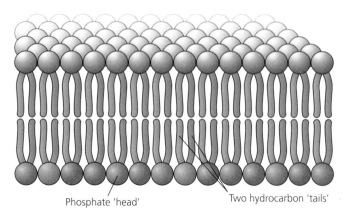

Phosphate 'head'

Two hydrocarbon 'tails'

Figure 1.12 Phospholipids form double layers when surrounded by water

Testing for lipids

The **emulsion test** is used to test for lipids. First, dissolve the test substance in ethanol and filter. Then add water to the filtrate. If the test is positive, the substance will turn cloudy/milky because an emulsion has been formed. An emulsion is a suspension of lipid/alcohol droplets in water.

Now test yourself

5 Describe how you would test a sample of cake for the presence of lipids.

Answer on p. 108

General properties of proteins

Proteins such as enzymes, antibodies and hormones are vital compounds in all living organisms. Their functions include holding your body together; allowing you to move, digest and absorb your food; controlling your body chemistry; and fighting off disease. Proteins are large, complex molecules that always contain the elements carbon, hydrogen, oxygen and nitrogen.

Amino acids

Amino acids are the **monomers** from which proteins are made. Most amino acids have names that end in –*ine* such as proline, valine and serine. All of them have the same basic formula, which you may be asked to draw (Figure 1.13).

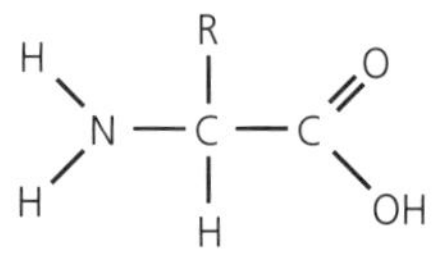

Figure 1.13 A basic amino acid

As you might expect from the name, there is an amino part and an acid part:
● the amino group is written as $-NH_2$
● the acid group is written as $-COOH$

It is the R group that is different. There are 20 different amino acids, so there are 20 different R groups. For example, in glycine the R group is simply a hydrogen atom, whereas in alanine the R group is CH_3.

Amino acids join by **condensation reactions**, forming **peptide bonds** in the process. There are two amino acids in a **dipeptide** (Figure 1.14), three in a tripeptide and many in a **polypeptide**. A **protein** is made from one or more polypeptides. A haemoglobin molecule, for example, is made from four polypeptides.

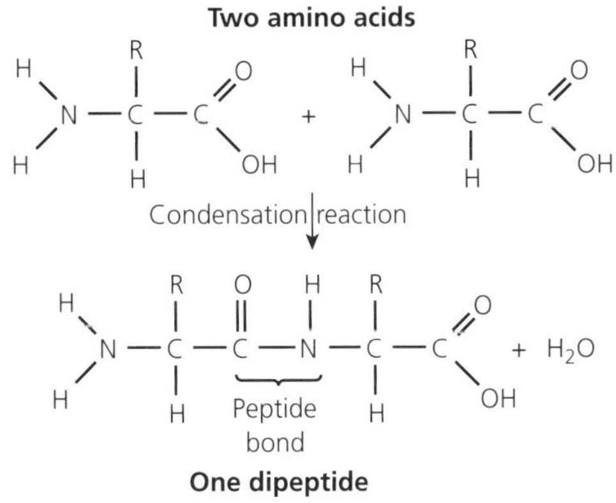

Two amino acids

Figure 1.14 How a dipeptide is formed

A **peptide bond** is the bond between two amino acids.

A **dipeptide** is formed when two amino acids are joined together by a peptide bond.

A **polypeptide** is a chain of many amino acids joined together by peptide bonds.

Exam tip

You don't need to remember the names of the different amino acids, but you should learn their general structure.

Exam tip

R does not stand for an element. Think of R as the **r**est of the molecule.

Revision activity

Draw a molecule of the amino acid alanine.

Exam tip

A dipeptide has the backbone N – C – C – N – C – C. You can use this to check that you have drawn it correctly. Longer peptides all have the same backbone.

There is an infinite variety of proteins. Amino acids can join in any order; some may be repeated and others left out completely. Having 20 different monomers is the key to their variety. If there are 20 different amino acids, there must be 400 (20^2) different dipeptides and 8000 different tripeptides. So there can be a different enzyme for every reaction, a different antibody for every disease etc.

Revision activity

Using a whiteboard or blank piece of paper, draw two glucose molecules side by side. Highlight the atoms that will be involved in a condensation reaction and then draw the resulting disaccharide. Repeat this activity for two amino acids.

Protein structure

REVISED

Proteins are large, complex molecules so we divide the study of their structure into four levels (Figure 1.15).

1 **Primary structure** is the sequence of amino acids, such as valine – serine – proline – valine. Insulin, for example, is a small protein consisting of 51 amino acids. Many proteins have hundreds.

2 **Secondary structure** is the shape formed when the chain of amino acids becomes folded and coiled. The two most common secondary structures are an α-helix (a spiral shape) and a β-sheet (pleated like a folded sheet of paper).

3 **Tertiary structure** is the overall shape of the amino acid chain, i.e. the whole polypeptide. When in water, a wide variety of forces combine to twist, fold and bend the polypeptide into its most stable shape. There are many different areas of secondary structure within the tertiary structure.

4 **Quaternary structure** occurs when the protein has more than one polypeptide chain. If a protein is made from only one polypeptide chain, it does not have a quaternary structure.

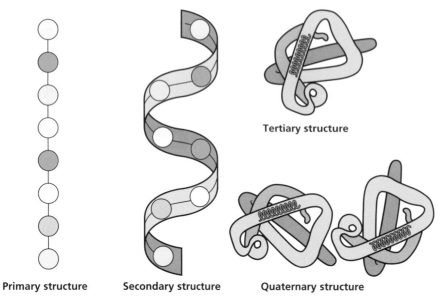

Primary structure   Secondary structure   Quaternary structure

Tertiary structure

Figure 1.15 The four levels of protein structure

Protein function

REVISED

Proteins can be split into two main groups: globular or fibrous.

Globular proteins are generally rounded in shape. They tend to have a chemical function. Examples include:
- enzymes (see p. 17)
- membrane proteins that control the movement of ions and other substances in and out of the cell (see p. 39)
- hormones such as insulin (some hormones are proteins, others are not)
- haemoglobin (see p. 66)
- antibodies to help fight disease (see p. 45)

Fibrous proteins are usually long, thin molecules that generally have a structural function. Examples of fibrous proteins include:
- collagen, which gives strength to tissues such as bone, tendon and ligaments
- keratin, which gives strength to skin, hair and nails
- actin and myosin, which make muscle contract

Generally, the shape of globular proteins is maintained by relatively weak forces such as **hydrogen bonds** and **ionic bonds**. In contrast, big tough fibrous proteins rely more on strong **disulfide bridges**.

Now test yourself

TESTED

6 Which elements are contained in the following?
 (a) carbohydrates
 (b) lipids
 (c) proteins
7 Which of these are polymers?
 proteins   triglycerides   glucose   sucrose   starch   glycogen   phospholipids

Answers on p. 108

Testing for proteins

The **biuret test** is a biochemical test used for detecting the presence of peptide bonds. First dissolve the test substance in water. Then add the biuret reagent (a mixture of copper sulfate and sodium hydroxide). A change in colour from blue to lilac/purple indicates the presence of protein.

Many proteins are enzymes

Enzymes are central to living things. Cells can be thought of as tiny units of controlled chemical reactions and it is the enzymes, together with hormones, that do the controlling. The reactions of the body are given the general name **metabolism**. Enzymes are named by adding *–ase* to the name of the substrate, so lactase breaks down lactose. Often the full name of the enzyme describes the reaction it catalyses. For example, glycogen synthetase makes (synthesises) glycogen.

Enzymes may be **intracellular** (working inside cells) or **extracellular** (working outside cells).

> **Intracellular** proteins work inside cells.
>
> **Extracellular** proteins work outside cells.

Tertiary structure

Enzymes are globular proteins. They have a precise shape — their **tertiary structure**. The substance an enzyme works on is called the **substrate**. There is a part of the enzyme's surface called the **active site** into which the substrate fits. The active site and the substrate are **complementary** — the substrate fits into the active site, partly because it is the right shape and partly because the chemical charges match. The **specificity** of an enzyme refers to its ability to catalyse just one reaction or type of reaction. Only one particular substrate molecule will fit into the active site of the enzyme molecule.

> The **tertiary structure** is the overall shape of the enzyme. Globular proteins are proteins which consist of polypeptide chains that are folded so that the molecule is roughly spherical and has a compact overall shape.

Enzymes as catalysts

Enzymes are catalysts, so they speed up chemical reactions without being altered themselves. For any reaction to take place, the reactant molecules must collide and achieve the **transition state** — one in which the existing bonds are strained. After this, the existing bonds will break and new ones will form as new products are created.

Enzymes speed up reactions because they **lower the activation energy** needed to achieve the transition state (Figure 1.16). This is achieved by enabling the reaction to take a slightly different pathway by forming an **enzyme–substrate complex**. This complex alters the bonding in the substrate, enabling the bonds to be broken more easily.

> **Exam tip**
>
> In exam questions about enzymes, examiners expect to see you using the correct language, so use terms such as *tertiary structure*, *collisions*, *active site*, *enzyme–substrate complex*, *complementary* and *denatured*.

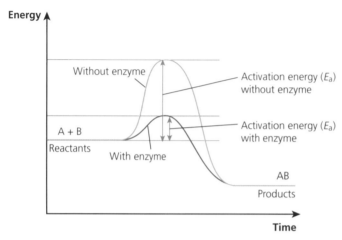

Figure 1.16 The effect of enzymes on activation energy

Now test yourself

8 Explain how enzymes are able to speed up chemical reactions.
9 On Figure 1.16, label the point at which the transition state is achieved.

Answers on p. 108

The lock and key and induced-fit models

The lock and key model states that the active site and the substrate are an exact match — they fit together perfectly (Figure 1.17). The active site is the lock and it only fits one key — the substrate. They come together to form an enzyme–substrate complex. Once formed, the reaction can be completed.

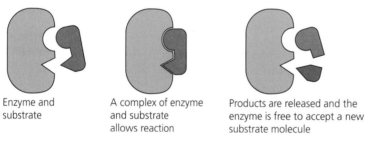

Enzyme and substrate

A complex of enzyme and substrate allows reaction

Products are released and the enzyme is free to accept a new substrate molecule

Figure 1.17 The lock and key model of enzyme action

The **induced-fit model** is slightly different from the lock and key hypothesis. The active site does not exactly match the substrate, but it alters its shape slightly when the substrate attaches. It is as if the active site moulds itself around the substrate (Figure 1.18).

> The **induced-fit model** is a hypothesis that modifies the lock and key model. It helps to explain how enzymes are specific to their substrate.

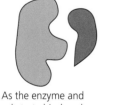

As the enzyme and substrate bind, a change of shape occurs

The reaction proceeds as the enzyme and substrate bind

Products are released and the enzyme returns to its original shape

Figure 1.18 The induced-fit model of enzyme action

Most scientists now accept that the induced-fit model is a more accurate model of what really happens. The lock and key hypothesis suggests that the active site is rigid, but we know from the action of non-competitive inhibitors that the shape of active site can change. Techniques such as computer modelling have further supported the idea that the active site is flexible and that the catalysis is brought about by a complex interaction of the substrate and the amino acids at the active site.

Typical mistake

The active site and the substrate are *not* the same shape. They are complementary — one fits into the other.

Now test yourself

TESTED

10 Usually, one enzyme catalyses just one reaction. Explain why enzymes are so specific.
11 Explain how the lock and key model of enzyme action differs from the induced-fit model.

Answers on p. 108

The effects of surrounding conditions on enzyme activity

REVISED

Enzyme concentration

The higher the **enzyme concentration**, the greater the rate of reaction until substrate becomes the limiting factor. In living cells, however, enzymes exist in active and inactive forms. An enzyme is converted into its active form — effectively increasing its concentration — when the product it makes is needed. When the product is no longer needed, the enzyme is deactivated, effectively lowering its concentration again. It is a really clever self-regulating mechanism.

Substrate concentration

In a similar way to enzyme concentration, Figure 1.19 shows that the more substrate there is, the faster the enzyme will work until all the active sites are full all the time. After that, no matter what the **substrate concentration**, the reaction will not go any faster. All enzymes have a maximum rate at which they can work.

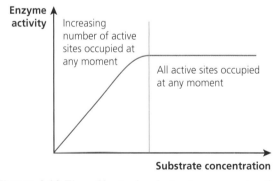

Figure 1.19 The effect of substrate concentration

Competitive and non-competitive inhibitors

Inhibitors are substances that slow down or stop enzyme action:
- **Competitive inhibitors** (Figure 1.20) are similar in shape to the substrate. They fit into the active site but cannot be converted into the product, so they simply get in the way.

- **Non-competitive inhibitors** (Figure 1.21) bind to the enzyme away from the active site, but they alter the shape of the enzyme so that the substrate cannot fit into the active site. Effectively, non-competitive inhibitors switch off enzymes. If the inhibitor is removed, the enzyme functions as normal.

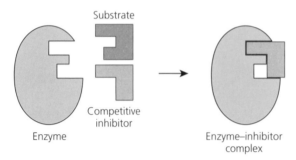

Figure 1.20 A competitive inhibitor competes with substrate molecules for the active site of the enzyme

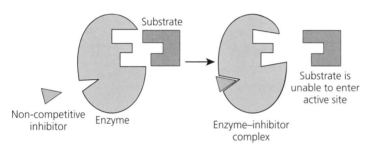

Figure 1.21 Non-competitive inhibitors bind to the enzyme somewhere other than the active site. This causes the active site to change shape

The key difference between the two types of inhibitor is that the effects of competitive inhibitors can be overcome by adding more substrate. It is simply a matter of improving the chances of a collision between enzyme and substrate compared with enzyme and inhibitor. With non-competitive inhibitors, on the other hand, it does not matter how much substrate is added — nothing can fit into the active site so there is no activity.

pH

The **pH** scale is a measure of acidity. On a scale of 1 to 14, pH 7 is neutral. A pH lower than 7 is acidic — there are a lot of H^+ ions. A pH of more than 7 is basic — there are more OH^- ions.

Every enzyme has an optimum pH. Most enzymes work inside cells and their optimum pH is around neutral. Some enzymes in the digestive system are exceptions; the stomach enzymes work best at around pH 2, whereas those that work in the small intestine have their optimum at about pH 8.

At optimum pH, the positive and negative charges on the active site and substrate are complementary. Away from this pH, the H^+ or OH^- ions neutralise the charges so that enzyme and substrate are no longer complementary. In addition, extremes of pH can denature enzymes.

> **Exam tip**
>
> If the hydrogen ion concentration of a solution is known, the pH can be calculated by substituting the hydrogen ion concentration into this formula:
>
> $$pH = -\log_{10}[H^+]$$

Temperature

Figure 1.22 shows the relationship between enzymes and **temperature**. As the temperature increases, the rate of reaction increases because all the molecules bounce around faster and there is more chance of a collision between the enzyme and the substrate. Therefore, more enzyme–substrate complexes form, resulting in a product being formed more quickly.

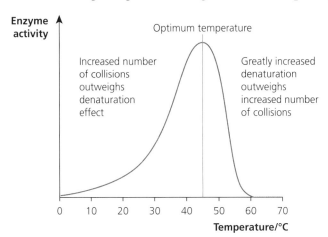

Figure 1.22 As temperature increases, the rate of reaction increases until the enzyme becomes denatured. It is often said that enzymes are denatured above 37°C, but most are more tolerant of heat. Individual enzymes have different optimums, but many are in the 45–55°C region

However, when the temperature gets too high, the enzyme molecules vibrate more vigorously and the weaker bonds, such as hydrogen bonds, break. The shape of the enzyme changes and the active site and substrate are no longer complementary. The enzyme is denatured and this process is permanent. Lowering the temperature will not make any difference — the enzyme will not revert back to normal.

Now test yourself

TESTED

12 Describe what happens when an enzyme is denatured. Make sure you use precise, A-level language.

Answer on p. 108

Nucleic acids are important information-carrying molecules

In this section we will look at the basic structure of the nucleic acids. The role of nucleic acids in making proteins is covered later in the specification and can be found on pp. 89–94.

The structure of DNA and RNA

REVISED

DNA

Deoxyribonucleic acid (DNA) has two vital properties:
- it holds the **genetic information** for making all the proteins that an organism needs
- it can copy itself exactly, time after time (replication — see p. 86)

You cannot have life without a molecule that can do this.

> **Deoxyribonucleic acid (DNA)** is an information-carrying molecule that forms the genetic material in all living organisms.

DNA molecules are large **polynucleotide chains** formed when **nucleotides** bind together in a long chain. The bonds are formed by **condensation** and are called **phosphodiester bonds**. The polynucleotide chains in DNA are like a twisted ladder called a **double helix** (Figure 1.23). The molecule develops a natural twist that makes it more stable. The two sides of the ladder are made from alternating sugar–phosphate backbones, held together by **hydrogen bonds** between **base pairs** (Figure 1.24). There is one complete turn of the molecule for every 10 or so base pairs.

Figure 1.23 The double helix that forms when two polynucleotide strands twist around each other

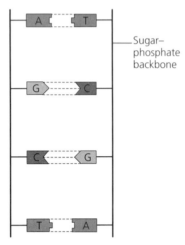

Figure 1.24 Part of a DNA molecule, with the sugar–phosphate backbones shown as single lines

Each nucleotide has three components (Figure 1.25):
- a **pentose** sugar (**deoxyribose**) — this is a five-carbon sugar, usually drawn as a pentagon
- a **phosphate group** — a PO_4^- ion that gives DNA a negative charge
- a **nitrogen-containing organic base** — one of four: **adenine** (A), **cytosine** (C), **guanine** (G) or **thymine** (T)

Figure 1.26 shows a single polynucleotide strand. Note how the pentoses and the phosphates form a sugar–phosphate backbone.

Most bonds in DNA are covalent bonds, which are very strong and help to make DNA stable. However, the molecule cannot do its job if the bases do not come apart, so they are joined by relatively weak hydrogen bonds. The two strands of the DNA molecule must come apart for both replication and protein synthesis.

The two sides of the DNA molecule are joined by the bases, which are **specific**: A can only bond to T, and C can only bond to G. There are two hydrogen bonds between A and T (A$=$T) and three between C and G (C$\equiv$G).

Figure 1.27 shows part of a molecule of DNA. You should be able to identify the nucleotides, the sugar–phosphate bonds joining the nucleotides in one polynucleotide strand and the hydrogen bonds between **complementary** base pairs that are linking the two polynucleotide strands. As the two strands run in opposite directions, this is called antiparallel.

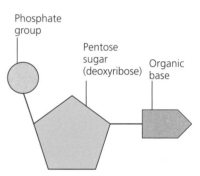

Figure 1.25 The structure of a single DNA nucleotide

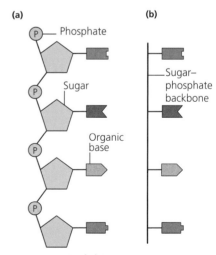

Figure 1.26 (a) Part of a single polynucleotide strand. **(b)** A simpler way to represent the same polynucleotide strand

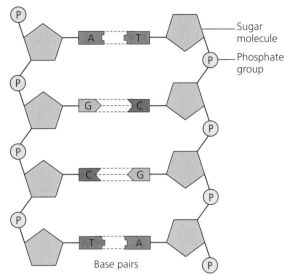

Sugar molecule

Phosphate group

Base pairs

Figure 1.27 The overall structure of a DNA molecule

TESTED ☐

Now test yourself

13 If the base sequence on one strand of a DNA molecule reads AACTAGGTA, what will the base sequence read on the opposite strand?

Answer on p. 108

Answer on p. 108

RNA

There are three types of **ribonucleic acid (RNA)** molecule:

- messenger RNA (mRNA) — think of them as mobile copies of genes
- transfer RNA (tRNA) — to bring the right amino acids to the ribosome
- ribosomal RNA (rRNA) — makes up the body of the ribosome

You will learn about the roles of mNRA and tRNA later, on pp. 89–94.

Like DNA, RNA molecules are polymers of nucleotides, but there are key differences. RNA molecules:

- are single-stranded
- are shorter then DNA
- have the sugar ribose, not deoxyribose
- have the base uracil (U) instead of thymine (T)

> **Ribonucleic acid (RNA)** is a type of nucleic acid similar to DNA. There are three types of RNA.

DNA replication

REVISED ☐

In the human body, most cells are not dividing so there is no need for the DNA to be replicated. However, if the cell is going to divide, the DNA must first be copied otherwise the resulting daughter cells will only contain half the genetic material. This ensures **genetic continuity** between generations of cells.

The key steps involved in DNA replication are as follows (Figure 1.28):

1 The enzyme **DNA helicase** attaches to the DNA molecule, breaks the **hydrogen bonds** between **complementary bases** in the two **polynucleotide strands** and **unwinds the double helix** of the DNA molecule, producing two single strands.

1 Biological molecules

2 The enzyme **DNA polymerase** attaches to each strand. Each enzyme moves along its strand, catalysing the addition of new complementary **nucleotides** to the **exposed bases**. For example, wherever there is an exposed T base, an A base will be added. There is only ever one base that can be paired to the original. This is the key to keeping the code unchanged.

3 Sugar–phosphate bonds are formed and the double helix re-forms, so now there are two identical strands.

In each new molecule of DNA, half is original (it has been conserved) and half is new. This is what we mean by **semi-conservative replication**.

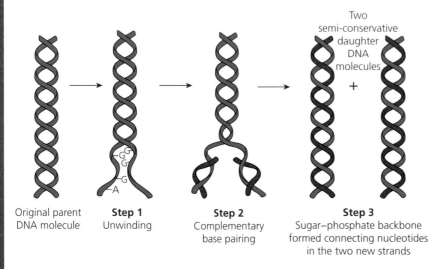

Original parent DNA molecule

Step 1 Unwinding

Step 2 Complementary base pairing

Step 3 Sugar–phosphate backbone formed connecting nucleotides in the two new strands

Two semi-conservative daughter DNA molecules +

Figure 1.28 DNA replication

> **Typical mistake**
>
> Don't state that bases are added during DNA replication — it should be nucleotides. A nucleotide is a base with a sugar and a phosphate attached.

Now test yourself

TESTED

14 List four components needed for DNA replication.
15 Which bonds are broken by the enzyme DNA helicase?
16 In which part of the cell does DNA replication take place?
17 Explain what is meant by the term *semi-conservative replication*.

Answers on p. 108

ATP

The structure of ATP

REVISED

Adenosine triphosphate (ATP) is a substance found in all living organisms. Its function is to deliver instant energy in usable amounts. All organisms respire all the time because they need a constant supply of ATP.

Structurally, ATP is a **nucleotide**, like those that make up nucleic acids (Figure 1.29). It consists of:

- a pentose sugar (**ribose**)
- a base (**adenine**)
- three **phosphate groups**, which are the key to its function

> **Adenosine triphosphate (ATP)** is a substance, found in all living cells, that is involved in the transfer of energy.

ATP is a relatively simple molecule that releases its energy by **hydrolysing** into **adenosine diphosphate (ADP)** and an **inorganic phosphate group**, which can be written as PO_4^- or P_i.

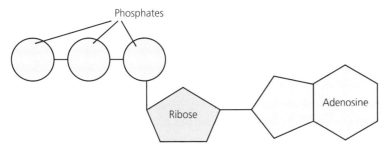

Figure 1.29 An ATP molecule

ATP:
- releases instant energy because it needs just one simple chemical step
- releases energy in usable amounts — if it released more energy than needed, the excess would be wasted as heat
- is a relatively small molecule so it can diffuse rapidly around the cell
- is often used to **phosphorylate** other molecules, making them more **reactive**
- is an unstable molecule that cannot be stored, so it must be resynthesised constantly

ATP synthesis and uses

ATP is made by the enzyme **ATP synthase**, a process that occurs in both **respiration** and **photosynthesis**. ATP is hydrolysed by **ATP hydrolase**, which is sometimes just called ATPase.

There is only a certain amount of ATP in a cell. It is constantly being broken down and needs to be resynthesised. In humans and all other warm-blooded animals that respire quickly, the weight of ATP produced each day is greater than the entire body weight. We have a relatively small amount of ATP but it is being constantly broken down and remade.

The balance of ATP and ADP/P_i in a cell is a bit like a battery. If it is all ATP, the battery is fully charged. If it is mostly ADP and P_i, the battery is run down and needs to be recharged by the process of respiration.

There are many processes that use ATP, but for exam purposes the three main ones are:
- muscular contraction
- active transport
- protein synthesis

1 Biological molecules

Water

Important properties

Water is the most common component of **cells** and therefore of whole organisms. There is no life without water. It is so fundamental to life that the search for life on other planets centres around searching for those that might have liquid water.

Water molecules are simple and most substances of a similar size are gases (Figure 1.30). However, water is a liquid at most of the temperatures found on Earth because its molecules are polar — they have areas of positive and negative charge. As a consequence, they act like mini-magnets and cling to each other. Hydrogen bonds form between adjacent water molecules, giving water several important properties:

- It is a metabolite in many metabolic reactions, including condensation and hydrolysis.
- It is an important solvent. Substances with a charge will dissolve in water. Sugars, amino acids and ions such as sodium, chloride, calcium and potassium are all soluble in water.
- It has a relatively high heat capacity, meaning that it acts as a thermal buffer. It can absorb a lot of energy before the temperature rises and lose a lot before the temperature drops.
- It has a relatively large latent heat of vaporisation, meaning that when water evaporates it has a powerful cooling effect with little loss of water through evaporation.
- Water molecules are cohesive (they attract one another) and so they cling together, forming continuous columns that can withstand great tension. This is important in xylem vessels in plants.
- The cohesive nature also results in surface tension, where water meets air.

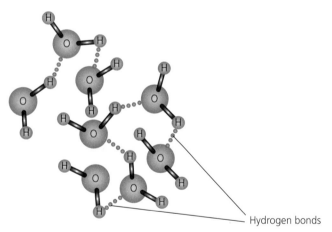

Figure 1.30 Water molecules

Inorganic ions

Important roles

Inorganic ions occur in **solution** in the **cytoplasm** and **body fluids** of **organisms**. Some — such as sodium, potassium and chloride — occur in high concentrations. Others — such as iodine, copper and zinc — occur in very low concentrations.

Each type of ion has a specific role, depending on its properties. These are particularly important:

- **Hydrogen ions** (H^+) affect the **pH**. Acidic solutions have an excess of H^+ ions, whereas basic solutions have an excess of OH^- ions. pH is a logarithmic scale, so a change from pH 5 to pH 4 represents a ten-fold increase in the concentration of H^+ ions, whereas a change from pH 5 to pH 3 represents a hundred-fold increase. Enzymes are very pH sensitive (see p. 20).
- **Iron ions** (Fe^{2+}) are a vital component of **haemoglobin**, where they form the centre of the haem groups that combine with oxygen (see p. 66).
- **Sodium ions** are vital in the **co-transport** of **glucose** and **amino acids** (see p. 44).
- **Phosphate ions** are components of phospholipids, **DNA**, **RNA** and **ATP** (see pp. 21–25).
- The most common ions are important in the regulation of water potential in cells and body fluids.

Exam practice

1 The two graphs show the effect of the two different types of inhibitor on the rate of an enzyme-controlled reaction.

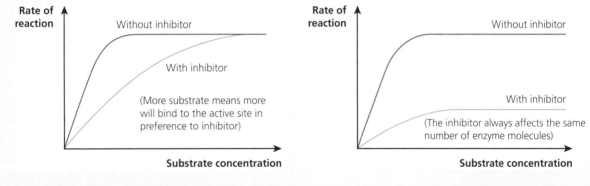

(a) Identify which graph shows the competitive inhibitor and which shows the non-competitive inhibitor. [1]

(b) Explain your answer to part (a). [2]

2 There are many different types of protein, but starch and glycogen are the same in all organisms. Explain why. [2]

3 Explain why you would not normally find glycogen in the blood of animals. [2]

4 A length of DNA was analysed and 21% of its bases were T (thymine). Calculate the percentage of the three other bases. [2]

Answers and quick quiz 1 online

Summary

By the end of this chapter you should be able to understand:

- That polymers are large molecules made from repeated monomers.
- The subunits that make up carbohydrates, lipids and proteins.
- How these subunits join to form larger molecules and the names of the bonds that join them.
- The importance of condensation and hydrolysis reactions.
- The way in which structure is related to function in starch, phospholipids and proteins.
- Why there is an infinite variety of proteins.

- The mode of action of enzymes.
- The factors that affect enzyme activity.
- The structure of DNA.
- The way in which DNA replicates.
- The differences between DNA and RNA.
- The structure of ATP and the way it releases energy.
- The properties of the water molecule and its importance in biology.
- The roles of inorganic ions, depending on their properties.
- The biochemical food tests for reducing sugars, non-reducing sugars, starch, lipids and proteins.

2 Cells

Cell structure

All living things are made from **cells**, which are tiny compartments of living tissue. Organisms such as bacteria, algae, yeast and amoeba are made from just one cell — they are **unicellular**. Large organisms are made from many cells — they are **multicellular**. Being multicellular is a huge advantage because it allows cells to specialise, which means that different cells have different functions.

Cell size

REVISED

In science, units of measurement usually go up or down in thousands, or 10^3:
- One thousandth of a metre is a millimetre (mm), or 10^{-3} m.
- One thousandth of a millimetre is a micrometer (μm), also called a micron, or 10^{-6} m.
- One thousandth of a micrometer is a nanometer (nm), or 10^{-9} m.

Cells and large organelles are measured in micrometers, whereas small organelles and molecules are measured in nanometers.

> **Exam tip**
>
> Remember:
> - 1 mm = 1000 μm
> - 1 μm = 1000 nm
>
> Avoid using centimetres in science — it just causes confusion.

> **Example**
>
> Calculations in biology
>
> The mitochondrion in the diagram is magnified 10 000 times. Calculate its actual size. [2]
>
>
>
> Answer
> (a) Measure the diagram. It is 55 mm long. Don't use centimetres — you will get confused.
> (b) Convert your measurement into micrometers. It is 55 000 μm.
> (c) Divide your result by the magnification.
>
> $$\frac{55\,000}{10\,000} = 5.5\,μm$$

> **Exam tip**
>
> You don't have to be a good mathematician to succeed in biology, but you do need to be numerate. You need to be able to do basic calculations and to recognise a silly answer when you see one.

> **Exam tip**
>
> Use this formula:
>
> $$A = \frac{I}{M}$$
>
> where:
>
> A is the **A**ctual size of the object
>
> I is the **I**mage size
>
> M is the **M**agnification
>
> You need to be able to rearrange this simple formula to work out A, I or M, depending on what the question requires.

> **Exam tip**
>
> Exam questions on scaling will sometimes give you a scale bar. You have to work out the magnification from the scale bar and then use it to work out the actual size of the object. For example, if the bar tells you that it represents 5 μm and you measure it as 10 mm on the page (⊢——⊣), you know that the magnification is 2000 (10 000/5). Think of it as 'How did 5 μm become 10 000 on the page? They must have enlarged it 2000 times.'

Two types of cell

There are two basic types of cell: eukaryotic and prokaryotic.

Eukaryotic cells (Figure 2.1) are big and complex. Organisms made from eukaryotic cells include animals, plants and fungi. In fact, every organism apart from bacteria is made from one or more eukaryotic cells. You might think that all cells are tiny, but in the great scheme of things eukaryotic cells are big and complicated.

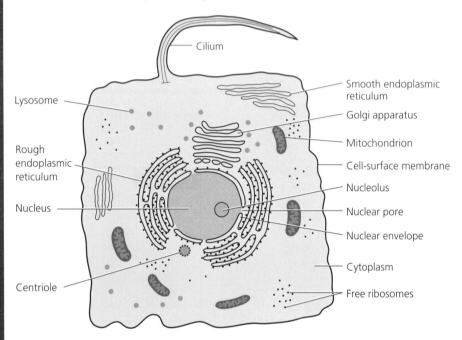

Figure 2.1 A eukaryotic cell (note that they do not all have cilia)

Prokaryotic cells (Figure 2.2) are small and simple. Bacteria have prokaryotic cells.

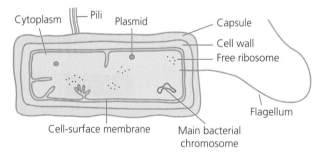

Figure 2.2 A prokaryotic cell

The structure of eukaryotic cells

Animal cells

Table 2.1 outlines the features of an animal cell. In this example, we will look at an epithelial cell from the lining of the gut, which is adapted for the absorption of digested food molecules.

Table 2.1 The main organelles found in an animal cell

Organelle	What it looks like	What is does	Relating structure to function
Cell-surface (plasma) membrane		Controls what enters and leaves the cell. It is a chemical barrier that has no physical strength	A variety of proteins, embedded in the lipid bilayer, control the movement of specific substances
Nucleus		Holds the DNA. Unless the cell is dividing, there are no visible **chromosomes** — the DNA is spread out and is known as chromatin. In eukaryotes, **DNA** is **linear** and is wrapped around organising proteins called histones. The nucleolus is a region of the nucleus where ribosomes are synthesised	Many pores to allow substances in and out
Mitochondria		Aerobic respiration. The energy in organic molecules is released and used to make ATP	Folds of inner membrane (cristae) give a large surface area for making ATP
Golgi apparatus		Modifies and activates ('finishes off') proteins made by the cell. Vesicles containing unfinished proteins are constantly being added to the forming face, while vesicles containing the finished product are constantly being pinched off the maturing face	The flattened cavities contain all the necessary enzymes
Lysosomes		Small spheres of membrane containing digestive enzymes. Used for destroying organelles or whole cells. White blood cells use them to destroy engulfed bacteria	Bags of lytic enzymes
Ribosomes	Ribosome diameter = 10nm Large subunit Small subunit Instructions to make a protein (written on an mRNA molecule)	Protein synthesis. Proteins are assembled according to the codes on the genes	Holds together all the components of protein synthesis

Organelle	What it looks like	What is does	Relating structure to function
Rough endoplasmic reticulum (covered in ribosomes)	Ribosome	Transport system in the cytoplasm. Newly synthesised proteins are stored and packaged into vesicles	Extends throughout the cytoplasm. Large surface area for the attachment of many ribosomes
Smooth endoplasmic reticulum (no ribosomes)		Synthesis of lipids, including steroids. Breaks down various drugs and toxins, including alcohol	The cavities contain all the necessary enzymes

Plant cells

Plants cells are eukaryotes, so they have all of the features seen in animal cells such as a true nucleus, linear DNA, mitochondria and endoplasmic reticulum. However, in general, plant cells tend to be larger than animal cells and have three additional organelles:

● a cell wall made from cellulose — all plant cells have them
● a large, permanent vacuole
● chloroplasts in certain cells

Cell walls

Cell walls are secreted by the plant cell itself. They are soft at first, but then harden to prevent any further expansion. The way the cell wall is laid down can lead to the cell being a particular shape.

Healthy plant tissue is usually turgid, which means firm. Think of crisp lettuce leaves. Plant cells absorb water and the cytoplasm swells until it pushes out against the cell wall, which prevents any further expansion. This is a turgid cell — it is a bit like a properly inflated football where the bladder pushes out against the leather. If a plant is short of water, the cytoplasm shrinks and turgor is lost, resulting in the plant wilting.

Vacuoles

Vacuoles are storage organelles found in plant cells. They might store food, nutrients or water. They can also store waste products to protect the rest of the cell. By the time a plant cell has stopped growing, the vacuole is usually very large and it can hold large amounts of water, organic molecules or pigments.

Chloroplasts

Chloroplasts are organelles with one function — photosynthesis — the details of which are covered in the A2 course. Chloroplasts are found in some plant cells, usually those that are exposed to light (Figure 2.3).

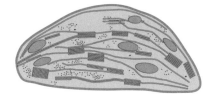

Figure 2.3 A chloroplast

Most of the plant's chloroplasts are concentrated in the palisade cells in the upper surface of leaves. The structure of a leaf allows the palisade cells to photosynthesise as efficiently as possible.

Chloroplasts are organelles that increase the surface area for the reactions of photosynthesis. Relating structure to function:

● chlorophyll molecules are attached to flat membranes called thylakoids
● stacks of thylakoids are called grana
● combining the two, there is a large surface area for light harvesting
● the flat, disk-like shape speeds up the diffusion of substances in and out

Exam practice answers and quick quizzes at **www.hoddereducation.co.uk/myrevisionnotes**

- the enzymes and other substances that turn carbon dioxide into sugar are found in the fluid (the stroma)
- starch grains allow sugars to be stored without lowering the water potential

Now test yourself

TESTED

1 Why are there no chloroplasts in the tissues of roots?

Answer on p. 108

Cells, tissues and organs

All plants and animals, by definition, are multicellular. The advantage of being multicellular is that cells can **specialise**, i.e. become adapted for different functions. Examples of specialised cells include neurones, spermatozoa and palisade cells.

A collection of specialised cells is known as a **tissue**. Examples of animal tissues include nerve, muscle and connective tissue. Plant tissues include palisade mesophyll, xylem and phloem.

An **organ** is a collection of tissues working together to perform a common function. Examples of animal organs include the eye, heart, lung and kidney, whereas plants have organs such as roots, leaves and flowers.

Organs are organised into **systems** that work together to perform a major function. Examples include the digestive, respiratory and reproductive systems.

The structure of prokaryotic cells (bacteria)

REVISED

The structure of prokaryotic cells is outlined in Table 2.2.

Table 2.2 The structure of prokaryotic cells

Feature	Details
Capsule	Some bacteria may have a layer of mucus outside the cell wall. This provides some protection from digestion by enzymes in the gut of animals and from drying out
Cell-surface (plasma) membrane	All living cells, including prokaryotic cells, have a cell-surface membrane
Cell wall	All bacteria have a complex cell wall, with more layers and components than the simple cellulose cell wall of plant cells. Prokaryotic cell walls contain a substance called murein (also known as peptidoglycan), which is a mesh formed from amino acids and sugars
Cytoplasm	A fluid in which most of the basic life functions occur, such as respiration
DNA	Bacterial DNA is always circular, i.e. the ends are joined together to form a loop. In every bacterial cell there is one main chromosome that contains all the genes essential for life, and several smaller plasmids that also contain useful genes. Bacterial DNA is not attached to organising proteins
Flagella (singular: flagellum)	A whip-like tail that is present in some prokaryotic cells to allow movement
Plasmid	Small loops of DNA. They contain genes that are useful rather than essential
Pili	Small, hair-like projections from the outer cell surface
Ribosomes	For protein synthesis. Bacteria have small, 70S ribosomes compared with the larger 80S ribosomes of eukaryotes

Viruses

Viruses are tiny, infectious particles (Figure 2.4). They are usually classed as **non-living** because they are not made of cells — they are **acellular** — and they only do one of the seven signs of life: reproduction. They do not feed, respire, excrete or grow. They can only reproduce themselves by infecting a living cell and using the host's organelles to make more virus particles.

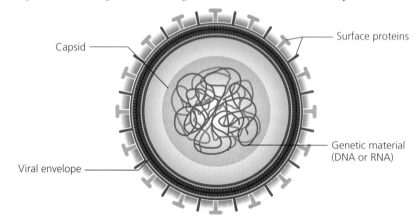

Capsid

Surface proteins

Genetic material (DNA or RNA)

Viral envelope

Figure 2.4 The basic structure of a virus

All viruses have:
- **genetic material** in the form of DNA or RNA. Viruses that contain RNA are called **retroviruses**
- a protein coat called a **capsid**
- **attachment proteins** that allow them to attach to end enter a cell

Now test yourself

2 State whether each of these describes a eukaryotic or a prokaryotic cell.
  (a) large; highly organised; lots of membrane-bound organelles
  (b) has a complex cell wall
  (c) contains endoplasmic reticulum
  (d) has plasmids

Answer on p. 108

Methods of studying cells

There are two basic types of microscope: optical (light) and electron.

Optical (light) microscopes

The microscopes used in schools and colleges are **light microscopes**, so called because they use light, focused by lenses. The power of microscopes is limited by the laws of physics, specifically the wavelength of light and electron beams. Most light microscopes have a maximum magnification of a few hundred and even the most expensive will not go much beyond 1500×.

Electron microscopes

Electron microscopes have greater magnification and resolution than light microscopes. They use a beam of electrons, focused by magnets. The wavelength of an electron beam is much smaller than the wavelength of light, so its potential to enlarge and show detail is much greater.

There are two types of electron microscopes commonly used in biology: **transmission electron microscopes** (TEMs) and **scanning electron microscopes** (SEMs). TEMs were developed first and work on the principal that electrons are transmitted through the specimen. With SEMs, electrons bounce off the surface of the specimen and images are produced by computers.

TEMs produce images that are two-dimensional. Specimens need to be thin, coated with a heavy metal (an electron-dense material) and observed in a vacuum. This means that it takes a while to prepare specimens and you cannot observe living material. On the other hand, SEMs are can study solid specimens, not just thin sections. They use computers to produce three-dimensional images. The resolution of TEMs is slightly higher than that of SEMs.

The best electron microscopes can magnify objects by as much as 10 000 000× and have a resolution of less than 1 nm. This means that at maximum power they can distinguish between individual molecules.

Now test yourself

TESTED ☐

3 Draw a table of the differences between transmission electron and scanning electron microscopes.

Answer on p. 108

Magnification and resolution

Many candidates confuse magnification and resolution.

- **Magnification** is how many times the image has been enlarged. For example, if an image says 20 000×, it is 20 000 times larger than it is in reality. Magnification can be calculated using this formula:

$$\text{magnification} = \frac{\text{size of image}}{\text{size of real object}}$$

See p. 29 for more information on how to use this formula.

- **Resolution** means detail. It is defined by how close together two objects have to be before they are seen as one. For example, a resolution of 1 μm means that two objects separated by less than 1 μm will appear to be one object.

> **Magnification** is the ratio of the image size to the object size.
>
> **Resolution** is the ability to distinguish two separate points that are close together.

Typical mistake

When talking about electron microscopes, candidates often mention magnification but forget about resolution, which is the key property.

Cell fractionation and ultracentrifugation

Cell fractionation involves separating the different components of cells. For example, you might want to study the mitochondria in a piece of liver or the chloroplasts in spinach. How do you get samples of pure organelles? The basic process is as follows:

1 Add an ice-cold, isotonic buffer to the tissue. When cells are broken up, chemicals that do not normally come into contact will mix, so a solution is needed that is:
  ○ **ice cold** to minimise unusual reactions, especially ones involving enzymes
  ○ **isotonic** to prevent organelles swelling up or shrinking due to osmosis
  ○ a **buffer** to prevent any damaging pH changes
2 Homogenise the piece of tissue (put it into a blender). This breaks up the cell membranes and cell walls, if present, so you get a 'soup' of organelles.
3 Filter the resulting mixture to get rid of any large lumps of unbroken cells and cell debris.
4 Spin the mixture in a centrifuge. This creates a super-gravitational field that causes organelles to separate according to their density. The

mixture is spun relatively slowly at first. This causes the nuclei to sediment out, forming a solid **pellet** of sediment at the bottom of the tube. The rest of the organelles are still suspended in the fluid, called the **supernatant**.

5 If the supernatant is spun again at higher speed (**ultracentrifugation**), the next densest organelles sediment out, which are the mitochondria. Increasing the speed separates out the lysosomes, endoplasmic reticulum and finally the tiny ribosomes.

All cells arise from other cells

Mitosis

REVISED

For multicellular organisms to grow and develop, cells must **divide** and then specialise. **Mitosis** is cell division that involves the **parent cell** dividing to produce two identical **daughter cells**, each with the **identical copies** of DNA produced by the parent cell during **DNA replication**. This means the cells are genetically identical to the parent cell and to each other.

> **Mitosis** is the division of cells to produce two genetically identical daughter cells.

Mitosis is divided into four key stages, as shown in Table 2.3.

Table 2.3 The four stages of mitosis

Phase	What it looks like	Main events
Prophase	Centromere; Spindle fibres; Two chromatids make up each chromosome	Chromosomes coil and become shorter and fatter, so that they are now visible with an optical microscope The nuclear envelope disappears Protein fibres form a **spindle** in the cell
Metaphase		The spindle fibres attach to the middle (**centromere**) of each chromosome The chromosomes line up so that they lie across the equator of the spindle
Anaphase		The centromere holding each pair of sister **chromatids** together divides The spindle fibres shorten and pull the chromatids to opposite poles of the cell The chromatids are now called chromosomes again
Telophase		The two sets of chromosomes group together at each pole and a nuclear envelope forms around each group The chromosomes uncoil, becoming chromatin again They are no longer visible with an optical microscope

Exam practice answers and quick quizzes at **www.hoddereducation.co.uk/myrevisionnotes**

The cell cycle

REVISED

The complete life of a cell, from the moment it is created until it splits again into two new cells, is called the **cell cycle**. Mitosis is only a small part of the cell cycle. The rest is known as **interphase**, when the chromosomes are copied and the genetic information is checked. During interphase, the cell also increases in size, produces new organelles and stores energy for another division. If the cell is going to divide again, DNA is replicated during interphase, just before the chromosomes condense and become visible.

Most cells are in interphase for most of the time. During interphase:
● the nucleus is intact — its membrane can be seen
● chromosomes are not visible — the DNA is spread out
● genes are being expressed — used to make proteins

The cell cycle is divided into four phases (Figure 2.5):
1 G_1 phase — the cell increases in volume as new cytoplasm is made. The cell prepares to replicate its DNA.
2 S phase — if the cell is going to divide, it enters the S phase in which it synthesises (replicates) its DNA.
3 G_2 phase — the cell continues to grow, and synthesises the enzymes and structures needed for mitosis.
4 M phase — the nucleus of the cell divides by mitosis.

The G_1, S and G_2 phases are collectively known as interphase. Once mitosis is complete, the cell divides into two cells during **cytokinesis** (Figure 2.6).

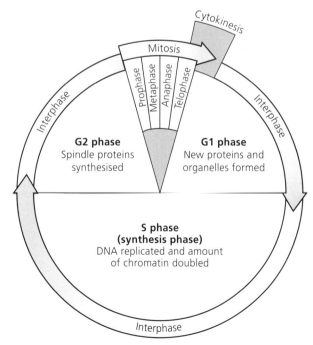

Figure 2.5 The cell cycle

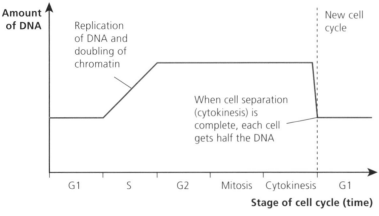

Figure 2.6 Changes in the amount of DNA during the cell cycle

Now test yourself

4 How many different nucleotides must be available in the cytoplasm in order for DNA replication to proceed?

Answer on p. 108

Cancer: when mitosis goes wrong

REVISED

Mitosis is a carefully controlled process so that cells only divide when they should. When the genes that control the cell cycle mutate, the result is uncontrolled division, resulting in a swelling or growth known as a **tumour**. There are two main types of tumour:

● Benign tumours are usually slow-growing and do not spread to other parts of the body. These are not classed as **cancer**.
● Malignant tumours grow much more quickly and often spread. Cells can break off and start up new tumours in other parts of the body. It is these tumours that are classed as cancer.

Cancerous cells go through the cell cycle faster than normal cells, so disrupting the cell cycle is an obvious target. The problem is that anything that affects cancerous cells also affects normal cells.

Broadly, there are three approaches to **cancer treatment**:

● Surgery — removal of the tumour. This may be difficult because of where it is located (e.g. in the head) and because it is difficult to remove all of the cancerous cells.
● Radiotherapy — radiation damages DNA.
● Chemotherapy — drugs are used to kill cancerous cells, preventing them from dividing or damaging them so that they kill themselves. There are several approaches to chemotherapy. Examples of drug action include:
  ○ blocking the enzymes involved in DNA synthesis in the G_1 phase
  ○ preventing DNA from unwinding so that replication is impossible
  ○ inhibiting the synthesis of new nucleotides
  ○ preventing the development of the spindle

The mitotic index

The mitotic index (*MI*) is a ratio showing the proportion of cells undergoing mitosis in a piece of tissue.

$$MI = \frac{\text{number of cells undergoing mitosis}}{\text{number of cells in sample}}$$

In practice, the number of cells undergoing mitosis is taken to be the number of cells that have visible chromosomes. This index is useful for determining when a tissue is becoming cancerous and for assessing the effectiveness of cancer treatment.

> **Exam tip**
>
> It is easy to get carried away and study cancer in too much detail. The specification states that 'Many cancer treatments are directed at controlling the rate of cell division'. If you have learnt the cell cycle and can make sense of graphs, you will be fine with questions about cancer treatments.

Binary fission in prokaryotic cells

REVISED

Bacterial reproduction is amazingly rapid and, in the right conditions, it can happen as often as every 10 minutes. It basically involves cells splitting in half and is known as **binary fission**. It involves:
● replication of the circular DNA and of plasmids
● division of the cytoplasm to produce two daughter cells, each with a single copy of the circular DNA and a variable number of copies of plasmids

Viral reproduction

REVISED

Being non-living and non-cellular, **viruses** do not undergo cell division. They can reproduce only by entering a host cell and taking over some of the cell's organelles, using them to make more virus particles. All viruses are basically composed of a protein capsule that surrounds some nucleic acid, either DNA or RNA. The genes contained in the nucleic acids provide the information for making new virus particles. Once complete, the new virus particles burst out of the cell and can re-infect new cells.

Transport across cell membranes

The fluid-mosaic model of membrane structure

REVISED

The basic structure of all cell membranes, including cell-surface membranes and the membranes around the organelles of eukaryotes, is the same. The **fluid-mosaic model** (Figure 2.7) is used to describe this structure. Described as 'protein icebergs in a lipid sea', the key elements are:
● a bilayer of **phospholipid** molecules
● cholesterol, which reduces the permeability and fluidity of the membrane, making it more stable
● **proteins** that float in the phospholipid bilayer. Some proteins are partially embedded in the bilayer — these are called extrinsic proteins. Others span the bilayer — these are called intrinsic proteins. Some proteins float freely in the bilayer, whereas others may be bound to other components in the membrane or to structures inside the cell
● **glycolipids** (sugars attached to lipids) and **glycoproteins** (sugars attached to proteins), which function in cell signalling or cell attachment

> The **fluid-mosaic model** is the basic structure of all membranes in a cell. Whenever you draw a cell, each line is a membrane.

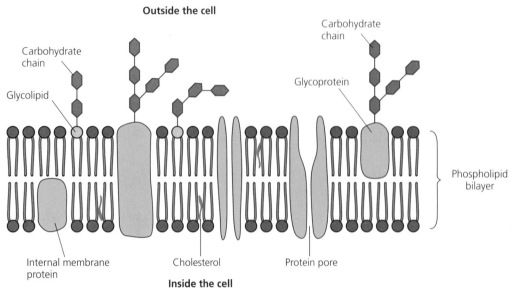

Outside the cell

Carbohydrate chain

Carbohydrate chain

Glycolipid

Glycoprotein

Phospholipid bilayer

Internal membrane protein

Cholesterol

Protein pore

Inside the cell

Figure 2.7 The fluid-mosaic model of membrane structure

What can and cannot get across membranes?

Small, simple molecules such as water, oxygen and carbon dioxide can pass freely across. Lipid-soluble molecules such as alcohol (ethanol), aspirin, steroid hormones and some vitamins can pass through the phospholipids. Small, water-soluble molecules such as glucose and amino acids can pass through protein pores. Ions such as sodium, potassium and chloride pass through specific membrane proteins. Large molecules such as proteins cannot pass through at all, except by endocytosis and exocytosis.

The difference between lipid-soluble molecules and water-soluble molecules is important in biology. As a general rule, ions and polar molecules (those with areas of positive and negative charge) will dissolve in water. Molecules that do not have a charge will dissolve in lipid.

Now test yourself

5 Suggest how fructose passes across cell membranes.

Answer on p. 108

Diffusion

Diffusion is the **passive transport** of substances down a **concentration gradient**, until they are evenly distributed.

In liquids and gases, particles are free to move and are constantly colliding with each other and changing direction (Figure 2.8). As a consequence, particles bounce around until they are evenly distributed. Diffusion is vital in gas exchange.

Examples of diffusion include:
● in the lungs, oxygen diffuses from the air into blood and carbon dioxide diffuses in the opposite direction
● in the gills, oxygen diffuses from water into the blood
● in leaves, carbon dioxide diffuses into palisade cells

> **Diffusion** is the net movement of molecules down a concentration gradient.
>
> A **concentration gradient** exists between an area of high concentration and an area of low concentration.

The rate of diffusion is affected by:
- surface area
- differences in concentration (or gradient) between the two areas
- thickness of the exchange surface between the two areas — often, this is the thickness of the membrane
- temperature — at higher temperatures, particles bounce around and spread more quickly

Fick's law is used to measure of the rate of diffusion. It states that:

$$\text{rate of diffusion} \propto \frac{\text{surface area} \times \text{concentration gradient}}{\text{thickness of the exchange surface between the two areas}}$$

In order for diffusion to be as fast as possible, the two top factors need to be as large as possible and the one at the bottom needs to be as small as possible. Looking at the lungs, for example:
- lots of alveoli provide a large surface area
- constant breathing and a good blood supply maintain the concentration gradient
- thin alveolar walls minimise the thickness of the exchange surface

Now test yourself

TESTED ☐

6 Explain why diffusion is faster at high temperatures.

Answer on p. 108

Facilitated diffusion

REVISED ☐

Facilitated means 'helped' or 'speeded up'. **Facilitated diffusion** is diffusion helped by a specific protein in the membrane. There are two basic types:

1 **Carrier proteins** transport medium-sized molecules into and out of cells. To do this, they usually have to undergo a change in shape. For example, the entry of glucose into the cells of the body is speeded up by having specific glucose carrier proteins.

2 **Channel proteins** have a hole running through the middle. They transport ions into and out of cells. Some are specific and only allow certain ions such as sodium or chloride to pass through; others are non-specific and allow several ions to diffuse. Some are open all the time and others have gates (gated channels) that can open and close.

Facilitated diffusion stops when equilibrium is reached. It *does not* move substances against a concentration gradient; nor does it need energy in the form of ATP.

Osmosis

REVISED ☐

Osmosis is a special case of diffusion in which water moves from a solution of higher water potential to a solution of lower water potential through a partially permeable membrane.

All substances that dissolve in water do so because they attract water molecules. A glucose molecule, for example, is surrounded by a layer of water molecules. The more glucose molecules there are in a solution, the more water molecules they will attract.

Randomly moving water molecules Membrane

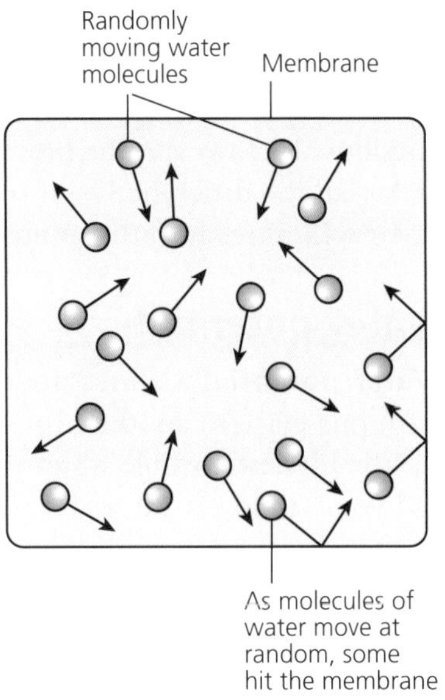

Figure 2.8 Like all particles that are free to move, water molecules bounce around at random, colliding and changing direction until they are evenly distributed

As molecules of water move at random, some hit the membrane

Osmosis is the net movement of water from a region of higher water potential to a region of lower water potential through a partially permeable membrane.

Osmosis happens whenever two solutions are separated by a membrane that allows the water molecules (but not the solute) to move. If there were no membrane, the solute would simply diffuse until it was evenly distributed. However, the presence of a partially permeable membrane makes all the difference — if the solute cannot move into the water, the water will move into the solute.

Water potential

Water potential is a measure of tendency of water molecules to move from one place to another. Imagine a beaker of pure distilled water. It has the highest possible water potential — zero. Add a spoonful of sugar and you will lower the water potential, i.e. make it more negative. It is a negative scale because all solutions have a lower water potential than pure water. The more sugar you add, the lower the water potential gets. Really concentrated syrupy solutions have very low water potentials (Figure 2.9).

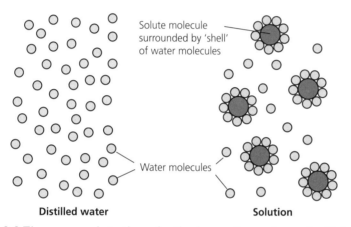

Figure 2.9 The more solute there is, the lower the water potential

Water potential is given the Greek letter Ψ (*psi*, pronounced 'sigh'). It is a measure of pressure and is measured in kilopascals (kPa). A weak solution might have a water potential of -50 kPa, whereas a more concentrated one might have a water potential of -300 kPa (Figure 2.10).

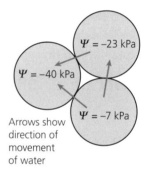

Figure 2.10 When cells of different water potentials are in close contact, water will pass to the ones with the lower values

> **Exam tip**
>
> Osmosis is the *net* movement of water. Water molecules will move in both directions but, overall, there will be more moving in a particular direction.

Now test yourself

TESTED ☐

7 A cell with a water potential of -200 kPa is next to one with a water potential of -250 kPa. Which way will the water molecules move? Explain your answer.

Answer on p. 108

Osmosis in cells

Osmosis is vital in biology because all cells contain a solution (cytoplasm) and they are all surrounded by a solution. In the case of mammals, all cells are bathed in tissue fluid. Cell membranes are freely permeable to water but not to solutes.

Animal cells

Think about what would happen if we added pure water to a sample of blood. The cytoplasm in the red cells has a lower water potential than the surrounding solution, so the cells would absorb water, swell up and burst. Animal cells have no cell wall and so burst easily.

> **Exam tip**
>
> You need to be able to answer osmosis questions in terms of water potential. Don't talk about 'more concentrated solutions' or 'less concentrated solutions'.

If we add sea water to a sample of blood, the opposite happens. Sea water is a concentrated solution of salt and it has a lower water potential than the red blood cells. Water is drawn out of the cells so that they shrivel up.

All of the cells in our body behave in the same was as red blood cells. Animal cells need to be bathed in a solution that is isotonic, which means that it has the same water potential as the cytoplasm. That is why we have kidneys — to get rid of the excess water or to conserve water when we have too little.

Plant cells

Plant cells are different from animal cells because they have a cell wall, so they cannot burst. If plant cells are placed in pure water, they absorb water and swell until the cell wall prevents any further increase. In this state the plant cell is said to be turgid. This is the normal, healthy state for most plant cells. Plant cells are covered in more detail on p. 32.

Now test yourself

TESTED

8 Most animals have organs such as kidneys to get rid of excess water. Explain why plants do not need these.

Answer on p. 108

Active transport

REVISED

Active transport moves molecules against a concentration gradient — from a low concentration to a higher one. This can only happen if energy is provided to drive the process. This energy is released from the **hydrolysis of ATP** (produced in respiration). Active transport also requires specific membrane proteins, usually referred to as **carrier proteins** or pumps.

> **Active transport** is the movement of molecules using metabolic energy in the form of ATP.

Some cells are adapted to maximise the rate of active transport. One example is the epithelial cells that line the small intestine, which show these adaptations:
- Microvilli are folds/projections in the cell-surface membrane. The more membrane there is, the more carrier proteins and channel proteins there are for active transport.
- Many mitochondria provide the ATP for active transport.

> **Exam tip**
>
> Candidates often lose marks by saying that cells have villi, but the correct term is *microvilli*.

Now test yourself

TESTED

9 If there were 100 molecules of a vitamin in the gut, how many molecules could be absorbed into the blood by the following means?
   (a) facilitated diffusion
   (b) active transport
10 (a) Which process in the cell produces ATP?
   (b) In which organelles does this process mainly take place?

Answer on p. 108

> **Exam tip**
>
> Candidates often state that epithelial cells have 'thin membranes', but they have normal membranes. It is the cells themselves that are thin, creating a short diffusion pathway.

> **Exam tip**
>
> If a question about cell transport says that a process is inhibited by a respiratory poison such as cyanide, you know it is an active process that needs ATP. Cyanide does not affect diffusion, facilitated diffusion or osmosis, but it does affect active transport.

Co-transport and the absorption of glucose

By far the most common monosaccharide in our diet is **glucose**, which is absorbed by cells lining the mammalian ileum (the small intestine) into the blood by a process known as **co-transport**. It involves both facilitated diffusion and active transport, and absorbs **sodium ions** (Na^+) at the same time (Figure 2.11).

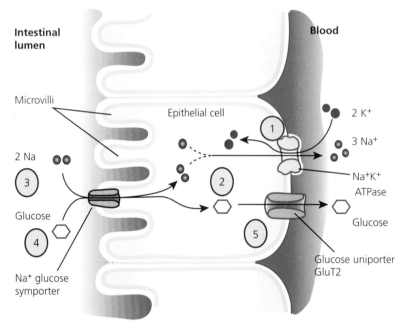

Figure 2.11 The absorption of glucose

1 Sodium is pumped out of the cell and into the blood by active transport.
2 This creates a low concentration of sodium inside the cell.
3 Sodium binds to the Na^+ glucose symporter (it is facilitated diffusion of sodium).
4 When sodium binds, so does glucose, so glucose is transported into the cell along with sodium.
5 There is a higher concentration of glucose inside the cell than outside, so glucose passes into the blood by facilitated diffusion (through the GluT2 membrane protein).

Now test yourself

11 Explain what is meant by the term *co-transport*.

Answer on p. 108

Cell recognition and the immune system

Cell recognition

All cells have proteins and glycoproteins on their surface. These molecules allow the cells of the immune system to tell the difference between self and non-self. Specifically, they allow the immune system to recognise:

● **pathogens** — disease-causing organisms such as bacteria and viruses
● **cells from other organisms** of the same species. Every individual has a unique combination of proteins on their cells, so a transplant from another individual will be recognised as foreign
● **abnormal body cells**. The immune system can recognise damaged cells, such as cancerous cells, and destroy them before a tumour develops
● **toxins** — potentially dangerous by-products of the metabolism of pathogens

Defence against disease

Defence against disease takes two forms:
● preventing the entry of pathogens into the body
● the **immune response**, which combats pathogens that have already entered the body

The immune response can be divided into two categories:
● **Non-specific responses** take place whatever the type of pathogen that gets in. The main non-specific responses are fever, inflammation (when an area becomes red, painful, hot and swollen) and phagocytosis.
● **Specific responses** involve the immune system recognising the type of pathogen that has entered and making exactly the right type of antibody to deal with it.

Now test yourself

12 List four of the body's barriers that prevent the entry of pathogens.

Answer on p. 108

Antigens and antibodies

Antigens are substances not normally found in the host's body, which stimulate the immune system into action. More specifically, antigens stimulate the production of a corresponding **antibody**. Antigens are usually proteins, polysaccharides or combinations of the two (glycoproteins). Non-self cells are recognised by the body because they have antigens on their cell-surface membranes. This means that phagocytes know which cells to attack. Pathogens are recognised because they are covered in antigens.

Antigens are molecules on the surface of cells that trigger an immune response.

An **antibody** is a protein made by lymphocytes in response to particular antigens. They have specific binding sites and are capable of acting against the pathogen.

Now test yourself

13 Would glucose be a likely molecule to act as an antigen? Explain your answer.

Answer on p. 108

All antibodies are Y-shaped proteins (Figure 2.12). Their molecules have:
- four polypeptide chains, two long and two short
- a variable region on the ends of the chains
- two antigen-binding sites, formed by the variable regions, that are complementary to the antigen

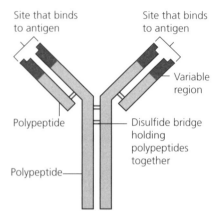

Figure 2.12 An antibody molecule

> **Exam tip**
>
> Remember two key points:
> - antibodies consist of four polypeptide chains, so they have a quaternary structure
> - different amino acid sequences give a different shape to the variable region

Antigen–antibody complexes form, which can neutralise the pathogen as follows:
- they label the pathogen as foreign — leading to phagocytosis
- they coat the pathogen so that it cannot invade a host cell
- they make pathogens stick together (**agglutination**) — again, preventing invasion of host cells

Now test yourself

TESTED

14 Explain the differences between antigens and antibodies.
15 Antibodies can be made only by white blood cells. Why is it not possible to simply make them in the lab, like aspirin or paracetamol?

Answer on p. 109

Phagocytes and lymphocytes

REVISED

The central component of the immune system is the vast array of white cells, which also have the general name *leucocytes*. The immune system is complex and it is easy to learn too much detail. You only need to know about these cells:
- **Phagocytes** (Figure 2.13). These cells usually have a lobed nucleus and carry out phagocytosis.
- **Lymphocytes** (Figure 2.14). These cells make antibodies. There are two basic types, **B lymphocytes** (or B cells) and **T lymphocytes** (or T cells). All white cells originate in bone marrow, but B cells are so called because they mature in bone marrow, whereas T cells mature in the thymus gland (in the chest). There are lots of different types of T cell, but the only two you need to know about are **helper T cells** (or TH cells) and **cytotoxic T cells** (also known as TC cells or killer T cells).

> **Exam tip**
>
> There are lots of other types of white cells including macrophages, neutrophils and basophils, but you don't need to know about these.

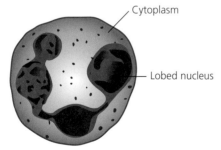

Figure 2.13 Phagocytes can be recognised by their lobed nucleus

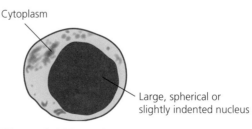

Figure 2.14 Lymphocytes can be recognised by their large round or kidney-shaped nucleus. T and B cells look exactly the same

Phagocytosis and the role of lysosomes

REVISED

Phagocytosis is a process in which white cells called phagocytes engulf and destroy bacteria and other foreign material that gets into the body (Figure 2.15). The steps are as follows:

1 The phagocyte recognises and engulfs the bacterium. The cytoplasm flows around and joins on the other side, leaving the bacterium enclosed in a vacuole called a phagosome.
2 **Lysosomes** move to the phagosome. Lysosomes are small vesicles (bags) of digestive enzymes.
3 The lysosome membrane fuses to the phagosome membrane to form a phago-lysosome. The enzymes digest the bacterium.
4 The remains of the bacterium are ejected from the cell, via exocytosis.

At the site of infection, phagocytes can engulf many bacteria. Eventually, a mixture of bacteria, dead tissue and dead white cells form a creamy fluid called pus.

> **Phagocytosis** is when a phagocyte engulfs and ingests a pathogen.

> **Exam tip**
>
> Make sure you have watched an animation showing phagocytosis.

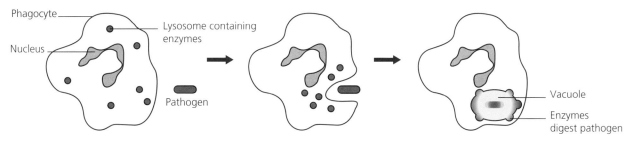

Figure 2.15 How a phagocyte ingests a pathogen

> **Exam tip**
>
> There is no need to be over-dramatic in answers about the immune system. It is not genocide. Words such as 'kill' and 'destroy' should be used sparingly. 'Annihilate' is definitely over the top.

> **Exam tip**
>
> Phagocytes don't 'eat' bacteria; they engulf and digest them. 'Eating' should only be used when describing animals that have a mouth and a gut.

The response of T lymphocytes to a foreign antigen

REVISED

When a particular pathogen gets into the body, the T lymphocytes respond as follows. This is known as the **cellular response**.

1 The pathogen is recognised as foreign and engulfed by a phagocyte.
2 This cell takes the antigens from the pathogen and 'displays' them on its membrane. It becomes an **antigen-presenting cell**.
3 The antigens are detected by helper T cells, which become activated.
4 In turn, the helper T cells activate three other types of cells:
   ○ phagocytes, which carry out phagocytosis (see above)
   ○ cytotoxic T cells (TC cells), which carry out cell-mediated immunity (see below)
   ○ B lymphocytes, which carry out humoral immunity (see below)

Cell-mediated and humoral immunity

The immune response takes two different forms: **cell-mediated immunity** and **humoral immunity**.

The cytotoxic T cells carry out cell-mediated immunity, meaning that the cell itself attacks the pathogen. TC cells attach to the pathogen and inject toxins into it, causing its death, or label the pathogen for phagocytosis. TC cells can also become **memory cells**.

The humoral response involves B lymphocytes which, when exposed to an antigen, form plasma cells. These cells produce and secrete antibodies to a specific antigen. A small number remain as memory cells. If cells carrying the same antigen enter the blood again, the memory cells recognise them and produce new plasma cells faster than before. A humour is a fluid, so humoral immunity means 'done by the fluid' and it refers to the fact that there are antibodies in the plasma (i.e. fluid).

Passive and active immunity

If the body is to survive exposure to a particular disease, it needs to be able to make antibodies in sufficient quantities to neutralise the pathogen. The problem is, we can only make enough antibodies if we have already been exposed to the pathogen. How do we survive that first exposure?

An unborn baby grows and develops in a sterile environment. Before birth, it gets antibodies across the placenta so that when it is born it already has some immunity passed on by its mother. After birth, the baby continues to acquire some immunity from its mother via her milk. Getting antibodies ready-made from the mother is called **passive immunity**. When the body makes its own antibodies, this is known as **active immunity**.

The primary and secondary immune responses

Primary response

As soon as we are born, we are exposed to a variety of pathogens. The immune system develops by **clonal selection:** at birth, we have millions of different types of B lymphocyte, each capable of making a particular antibody.

When a particular pathogen gets into the body for the first time, the T lymphocytes activate the B lymphocytes capable of making the right antibody, as described above. The B lymphocytes multiply into a large population of plasma cells and memory cells. This **primary immune response** generally takes too long to be effective in preventing symptoms, but it does create long-lasting memory cells.

Secondary response

The **secondary immune response** is the one you want. If we already have memory cells in place from the first exposure, a second exposure stimulates the memory cells to multiply rapidly into a clone of plasma cells, which can make the right antibody quickly enough to prevent symptoms developing (Figure 2.16). We are immune to a disease as long as we have the memory cells in place and can therefore produce the secondary immune response when exposed to a particular pathogen.

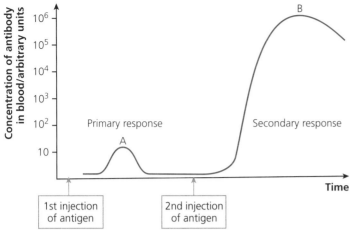

Figure 2.16 The primary and secondary immune responses

Exam tip

This uses a logarithmic scale, which allows a large range of values to be shown.

Now test yourself

TESTED

16 Suggest why breast milk is considered more preferable for young babies than powdered formula milk.
17 Explain what is meant by the term *memory cell*.
18 Outline the differences between the primary immune response and the secondary immune response.

Answer on p. 109

Antigenic variability in the flu virus

Antigenic variation refers to the mechanism by which an infectious organism such as a bacterium or virus alters its surface proteins in order to evade a host's immune response. The flu virus is well known for this ability: it rapidly mutates so that new strains, with new antigens, are constantly being produced. Any antibodies made against an old strain will not work against a new one.

Vaccines

REVISED

There are several types of **vaccination** that are used to provide protection for individuals and populations against disease:
● dead pathogens
● live but attenuated pathogens (ones that have been treated so that they cannot cause disease)
● purified antigens

Exam tip

The terms *vaccination* and *immunisation* mean the same thing.

Whatever the type of vaccine, they all contain antigens and stimulate the primary response so that the body has memory cells in place. If or when the actual pathogen enters the body, the memory cells multiply into plasma cells, which in turn produce antibodies in large enough quantities to fight the infection before symptoms appear.

Herd immunity

Herd immunity is the idea that you do not have to vaccinate everyone in order to stop an epidemic. You just have to vaccinate a large enough proportion of the population in order to break the chain of transmission, providing a measure of protection for individuals who are not immune.

HIV and AIDS

The structure of the **human immunodeficiency virus (HIV)** is shown in Figure 2.17. It is classed as a retrovirus because its genetic material is RNA. In order to reproduce, the virus must turn its RNA into DNA, transcription in reverse, so it possesses the enzyme **reverse transcriptase**.

HIV causes the symptoms of **AIDS** because it invades and reproduces inside a particular type of helper T cell, called a CD4 cell, killing them or preventing their replication. If left untreated, HIV infection reduces the helper T cell population to a level where they no longer activate other cells and the immune system is no longer effective. The body is left vulnerable to opportunistic infections and death is caused by pathogens that would normally cause little trouble.

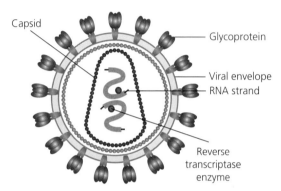

Capsid

Glycoprotein

Viral envelope

RNA strand

Reverse transcriptase enzyme

Figure 2.17 The HIV virus

Antibiotics work because they interfere with some aspect of prokaryote cell function while not harming eukaryote cells. Antibiotics do not work against viral diseases such as HIV because viruses do not have internal organelles or any metabolism that can be targeted.

Monoclonal antibodies

Monoclonal antibodies are useful in science and medicine because they are specific and bond with just one type of substance. They can detect minute quantities of a particular substance and are therefore important in **medical diagnosis**. For example, in pregnancy tests, antibodies detect very small quantities of the hormone hCG. The more sensitive the test, the earlier it can be done.

The problem is that large quantities of antibody are needed, but B lymphocytes do not grow well in culture outside the body. If B lymphocytes are joined with certain cancer cells, the resulting cells will divide again and again, while making useful amounts of the desired antibody.

In addition to diagnosis, monoclonal antibodies can be used as therapeutic agents because of their ability to seek out particular cells. For example, certain tumours may express a particular protein on their cell-surface membrane. If an anti-cancer drug is attached to the antibody complementary to these proteins, it will seek out and deliver the drug to exactly the cancerous cells that need to be targeted.

Ethical issues with vaccines and monoclonal antibodies

REVISED

The use of vaccines seems pretty uncontroversial, but there are issues:
- They may be produced using animal tissue such as eggs, so strict vegans may object to receiving them.
- In a pandemic (widespread outbreak), when vaccinations are urgent, who has priority?
- Should people have the right to say no to a vaccination? It is currently unlawful to force anyone to have a vaccination but, in refusing, is an individual putting others at risk?

The issues with monoclonal antibodies include:
- They are produced using live animals, usually mice. There is a need to induce tumours in the mice, which some people see as unacceptable.
- Monoclonal antibodies have been used successfully to treat life-threatening diseases, including some types of cancer. However, a number of trials involving the use of monoclonal antibodies to treat disease have been fatal.

The ELISA test

REVISED

The **ELISA test** (enzyme-linked immunosorbent assay test) is a sensitive test that uses monoclonal antibodies to detect particular substances, often antigens. The test usually involves particular enzymes and their substrates, an antigen–antibody reaction and a visible colour change.

Now test yourself

TESTED

19 Use your knowledge of herd immunity to explain why some people think that vaccinations should be made compulsory for all.

Answer on p. 109

Exam practice

1 The graph shows the results of nine cases of breast cancer in which a new combined chemotherapy and microwave treatment is compared with chemotherapy alone. The aim is to shrink the tumour so that it can be removed effectively by surgery without having to remove the whole breast.

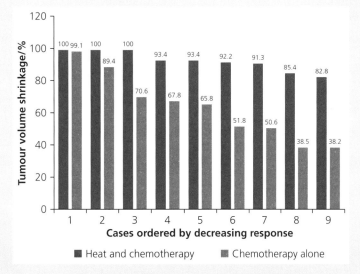

Source: www.ll.mit.edu/news/clinicaltrial.html

(a) What is meant by a tumour volume shrinkage of 100%? [1]

(b) In case 3, the breast tumour had an initial volume of 150 cm³ (estimated by ultrasound). What was its volume after chemotherapy alone? [1]

(c) Give two conclusions supported by the data. [2]

(d) Evaluate the conclusion that heat and chemotherapy treatment should be used in all cases of breast cancer. [3]

2 Antibodies are proteins. Explain how the structure of proteins allows them to form many different types of antibody. [2]

3 Explain the importance of antigens in the process of phagocytosis. [2]

4 Vulnerable people are offered a flu vaccine every winter.

(a) Suggest what is meant by the term *vulnerable*. [1]

(b) Explain why a new vaccine is needed each year. [2]

5 Use your knowledge of the primary and secondary immune responses to explain how vaccines protect people from disease. [2]

6 Monoclonal antibodies are used in pregnancy tests. Explain how the properties of antibodies make them useful in diagnostic tests. [2]

7 Suggest why a parent might object to their child receiving a particular vaccination. [1]

Answers and quick quiz 2 online

ONLINE

Summary

By the end of this chapter you should be able to understand:

- The structure and function of the main organelles in animal and plant cells.
- The structure and function of the main organelles in prokaryotic cells.
- The differences between eukaryotic and prokaryotic cells.
- The essential features of a virus.
- The principles of and differences between optical and electron microscopes.
- How to do calculations involving actual size, observed size and magnification.
- The principles of cell fractionation (how to get samples of pure organelles).
- The stages involved in mitosis.
- Interphase and the cell cycle.
- The relationship between the cell cycle and cancer, and its treatments.
- How to calculate a mitotic index.

- The basic structure of all cell membranes (the fluid-mosaic model of membrane structure).
- How substances move across cell membranes.
- The process of phagocytosis, including the role of lysosomes.
- The definitions of antigen and antibody.
- Antibody structure and the formation of an antigen–antibody complex.
- The cellular and humoral responses and the role of B lymphocytes and T lymphocytes.
- The difference between the primary and secondary immune response and the role of plasma cells and memory cells.
- Why the flu virus is so variable and the problems this causes.
- How vaccines provide protection against disease.
- What is meant by *herd immunity*.
- How HIV causes AIDS.
- Monoclonal antibodies and their uses.

3 Organisms exchange substances with their environment

Surface area to volume ratio

The relationship between the size of an organism and its surface area to volume ratio

REVISED

Size matters a lot in biology. All organisms need to exchange material with their surroundings. Generally, they need nutrients and oxygen, and need to get rid of carbon dioxide and other wastes. There are two basic rules:
- the amount of material an organism *needs* to exchange depends on its volume
- the amount of material it *is able* to exchange depends on its surface area

As an organism increases in size, its volume increases, it has more cells and so it needs more from its environment. However, its surface area does not increase as quickly as its volume, so the larger an organism gets, the more difficult it becomes to absorb enough substances over its outer surface. Table 3.1 and Figure 3.1 show what happens to surface area, volume and **surface area to volume ratio** as an organism gets larger.

> The **surface area to volume ratio (SA : V)** is the surface area of an organism divided by its volume. It is a key concept as the surface area must be able to provide sufficient oxygen through diffusion from the environment.

Table 3.1 The change in surface area and volume as an organism gets larger

Length of organism (l) (mm)	Surface area of organism ($6 \times l^2$) (mm²)	Volume of organism (l^3) (mm³)	Surface area to volume ratio
1	6	1	6 : 1
2	24	8	3 : 1
3	54	27	2 : 1
10	600	1000	0.6 : 1

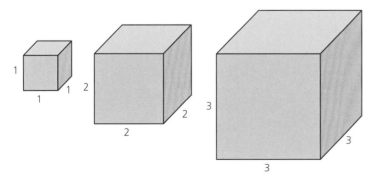

Figure 3.1 As the volume of a cube increases, its surface area to volume ratio decreases

So if an organism is large, it needs to develop adaptations that increase its surface area. There are two ways of doing this:

● having a flat or cylindrical (worm-shaped) body. This increases the surface area to volume ratio, so that all cells are a short diffusing distance from the outside
● having organs that increase the surface area, such as gills. This usually means that the organism also needs some sort of circulatory system to distribute the oxygen to the other parts of the body

Size and metabolic rate

REVISED

Metabolism is the general term for the biochemical reactions that occur inside an organism and **metabolic rate** is the speed of these reactions. In practice, metabolic rate is the same as the respiration rate and it can be determined by measuring the oxygen used by an organism.

Warm-blooded animals such as mammal and birds maintain a constant core body temperature, so they must balance heat generated with heat lost. Heat is generated by respiring cells and so the amount of heat made depends on an organism's volume. However, the amount of heat lost varies according to surface area. The smaller the animal, the higher its metabolic rate. This is because:

smaller animals have a high surface area to volume ratio

so they lose heat quickly to the surroundings

and have to respire quickly to generate heat to replace what is lost

so they must consume more food and oxygen per unit of body weight than larger animals

With a small mammal like a shrew, 99% of the food it eats is respired to maintain its body temperature. This is why it must consume almost its own body weight in food every day and its heart rate is over 800 beats per minute.

Now test yourself

TESTED

1 Suggest suitable units for measuring metabolic rate. Remember that you need to be able to compare organisms of different sizes.

Answers on p. 109

Gas exchange

Adaptations of gas exchange surfaces

Why do organisms need to exchange gas? It is all about **respiration** — the process that releases the energy locked in organic molecules such as glucose and lipids. All cells, in all living things, respire all the time. The process requires a constant supply of oxygen and produces carbon dioxide that needs to be eliminated. In addition, photosynthesising tissues need to absorb carbon dioxide and remove waste oxygen.

> **Exam tip**
>
> Ventilation and breathing refer to the same process, but respiration is different. Make sure you use the correct terms.

Single-celled organisms

Single-celled organisms are microscopic and have a very large surface area to volume ratio. They can exchange gas over their whole body surface. Gas exchange is rapid because the diffusing distances involved are very small.

Insects

If you look closely at an insect, you may see series of holes called **spiracles**, which are arranged in a row along the side of the body (Figure 3.2). Spiracles lead to breathing tubes (**tracheae**) that take air directly to the respiring tissues. The trachea branch out into a fine network of **tracheoles** which are so small and dense that they pass close to — and sometimes go inside — respiring cells. Diffusion through air is so fast that oxygen can be delivered quickly enough to supply the cells.

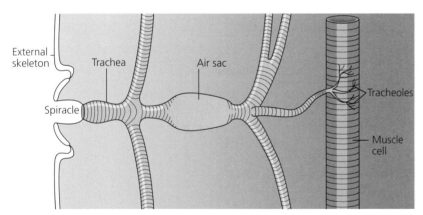

Figure 3.2 The tracheal system of an insect

Now test yourself

2 Explain why single-celled organisms such as amoeba do not need organs of gas exchange.
3 The abdomen of an active wasp can be seen pulsing. Use Figure 3.2 to suggest a reason for these movements.

Answers on p. 109

Minimising water loss

Most insects are **terrestrial** — they live on land. There are a few aquatic insects in freshwater, but virtually none in the oceans. Minimising **water loss** is important. Insects have two key adaptations:

- they have an exoskeleton made from waterproof **chitin**
- the spiracles can close when oxygen demand is low

Fish

It is not easy to breathe in water. Compared with air, water has much less oxygen but is about 800 times denser. It takes a lot of energy to move water. In addition, diffusion of oxygen and carbon dioxide is much slower through water than through air (Figure 3.3).

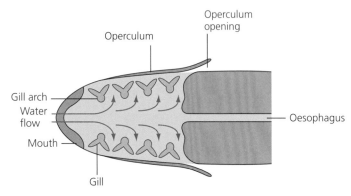

Figure 3.3 The flow of water over the gills of a fish

Gills are gas exchange organs that have evolved to overcome these problems. Instead of taking in water, stopping it and then forcing it out again — like we do with air — **fish** open their mouths and allow the water to flow in one direction, over the gills and out through the operculum (gill cover).

Gills have all the adaptations you would expect in gas exchange surfaces (Figure 3.4):

- Large surface area — each gill has several arches or **rakers** (typically 3 to 5) that support many **gill filaments**. On each filament are numerous **lamellae** — delicate flat structures that are the equivalent of alveoli.
- Small diffusing distance — the lamellae have very thin cells so there is a short diffusing pathway between water and blood.
- Efficient blood supply — a clever countercurrent system.

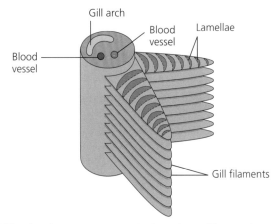

Figure 3.4 The basic arrangement of arches, filaments and lamellae

Exam practice answers and quick quizzes at **www.hoddereducation.co.uk/myrevisionnotes**

The countercurrent principle

The **countercurrent principle** involves two fluids flowing in opposite directions. This is an efficient way of maximising the exchange between the two fluids. In fish gills, the blood in the lamellae and the water flow in opposite directions. This means that there is always more oxygen in the water than in the blood. The key point to remember for exams is that this maintains a **diffusion gradient** (Figure 3.5).

(a)

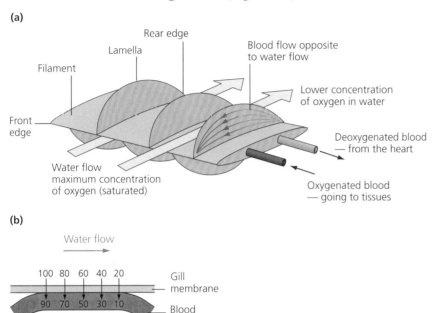

(b)

Figure 3.5 The countercurrent principle. (a) Water and blood flow in opposite directions. (b) Maintaining a diffusion gradient. The figures refer to the percentage saturation with oxygen

Now test yourself

TESTED

4 In fish gills, the blood in the capillaries flows in the opposite direction from the water passing over them. Explain the advantage of this system.
5 Use Figure 3.5 to predict what would happen if the water and blood were to flow in the same direction.

Answers on p. 109

Leaves

Plants need to exchange gas too. Leaves are organs of photosynthesis and, when it is light, the chloroplasts in the palisade cells need a supply of carbon dioxide and need to release the excess oxygen. Plant cells respire all the time, so when there is no light they need oxygen and make carbon dioxide. In order to maximise gas exchange, the leaves of a **dicot plant** have:

● loosely packed spongy mesophyll cells that create air spaces
● stomata — holes that allow direct access between the air spaces and the atmosphere

Xerophytic plants are adapted to living in dry (or arid) places. The following adaptations help them to reduce water loss:

● thick waxy cuticle on the leaves
● smaller leaf area
● stomata in pits
● hairy leaves
● rolled leaves

> **Exam tip**
>
> There are two types of flowering plant, monocots and dicots. Monocots are grasses and related species, white the dicots contain most other familiar groups.

The human gas exchange system

The **lungs** are organs that are adapted for gas exchange in air. Their function is simple: to get as much fresh air as possible in contact with blood. As you can see from Figure 3.6, the bronchial tree is a branching system of tubes that takes air to the **alveoli** deep in the lungs. All of the tubes are held open by rings of cartilage except the **terminal bronchioles**.

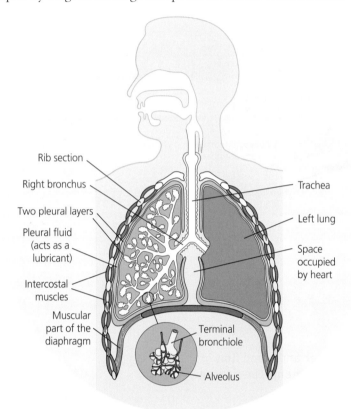

Rib section

Right bronchus

Two pleural layers

Pleural fluid (acts as a lubricant)

Intercostal muscles

Muscular part of the diaphragm

Trachea

Left lung

Space occupied by heart

Terminal bronchiole

Alveolus

Figure 3.6 The structure of the human gas exchange system

The alveolar epithelium

The **alveolar epithelium** is the surface over which gas exchange takes place. Its structure is related to function:

- Millions of alveoli provide a large surface area.
- The alveolar walls consist of flat cells called **squamous epithelium** that are as thin as possible. This makes the diffusing pathway as small as possible.
- The dense network of blood capillaries around the alveoli means that a lot of blood is in close contact with the air.
- The beating of the heart, along with constant breathing, makes sure that deoxygenated blood meets fresh air. This maintains a diffusion gradient.

All these features serve to make diffusion as fast and efficient as possible. The rate of diffusion of a substance across an exchange surface is inversely proportional to the thickness of the exchange surface.

The exchange of gases at the alveoli

The exchange of gases at the alveoli occurs by simple diffusion (Figure 3.7). Oxygen and carbon dioxide are small, simple molecules that pass easily through cell walls. There is more oxygen in the air than in the blood, so oxygen diffuses into the blood. There is more carbon dioxide in the blood than in the air, so this gas diffuses in the opposite direction.

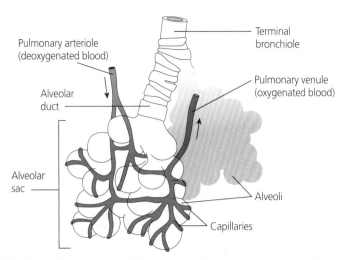

Figure 3.7 Alveoli are found at the end of the terminal bronchioles

Pulmonary ventilation, tidal volume and ventilation rate

Pulmonary ventilation rate (PVR) is the amount of air we inhale in 1 minute. It is calculated as using **tidal volume** and ventilation rate, as follows:

pulmonary ventilation rate = tidal volume × breathing rate

Typical values would be 0.5 litres for tidal volume and 14 breaths per minute, giving a pulmonary ventilation of 7 litres per minute.

Lung volumes are measured using a spirometer, which produces a trace like the one in Figure 3.8. When we exercise, our breathing undergoes a series of changes. Key points on the trace are labelled with the letters **A** to **E**:

- **A** to **B** shows normal, tidal breathing while at rest.
- **B** to **C** shows the effect of exercise — breathing is deeper and more frequent.
- **C** to **D** shows a return to normal after exercise.
- **D** shows the subject breathing out as far as possible.
- **E** shows the subject inhaling as much as possible.
- The difference in volume between **D** and **E** shows the vital capacity — the total usable lung volume
- The residual volume is the air that must remain in the lungs.

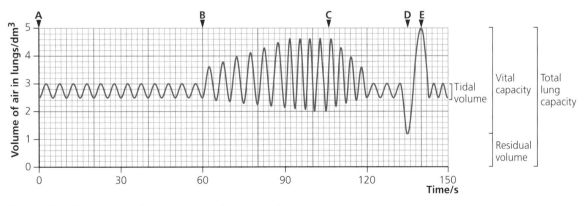

Figure 3.8 Changes in breathing during exercise

The mechanism of breathing

The lungs are spongy organs that simply fill with air and then empty again. They cannot do this on their own because they have no muscle. To inflate, they need the **intercostal muscles** and the **diaphragm**.

The **mechanism of breathing** is shown in Table 3.2. Inspiration is an active process — it requires energy. Expiration is largely a passive process. The lungs, diaphragm and intercostal muscles are all elastic. When stretched, they tend to go back to their original shape.

Table 3.2 The mechanism of breathing

Stage	Breathing in (inspiration)	Breathing out (expiration)
1	The external intercostal muscles contract, pulling the ribs up and out	The external intercostal muscles relax
2	The diaphragm muscles contract, flattening the diaphragm	The diaphragm relaxes. The abdominal organs (liver and intestines) push upwards
3	Their combined effect is to increase the volume of the thoracic cavity	The volume of the thoracic cavity decreases
4	This lowers the pressure in the thoracic cavity to below atmospheric pressure	The pressure inside the thoracic cavity increases
5	Atmospheric pressure forces air into the lungs	Air is forced out

The biological basis of lung disease

REVISED

The AQA specification does not list any particular lung diseases that need to be learnt in detail. However, it does say that students need to be able to interpret the effects of disease on gas exchange and/or ventilation, so it helps to know about the some common lung problems.

Emphysema

Fibrosis is a response to tissue damage. When normal body tissue such as lung, liver or heart becomes damaged, the body responds by producing connective tissue, commonly called scar tissue. Emphysema is fibrosis of the alveoli. Lung damage results from long-term exposure to irritants such as cigarette smoke and air pollution (Figure 3.9). When the delicate alveolar walls become damaged and replaced by connective tissue, the effects are:

● reduced surface area
● increased diffusing pathway due to the thicker walls
● decreased elasticity, so that the lungs cannot expand as much and it takes more effort to breathe out

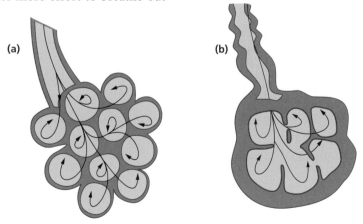

(a)　　(b)

Figure 3.9 (a) Healthy alveoli. (b) Alveoli in a person with emphysema

All three effects combine to make gas exchange less efficient. Emphysema is long-term, irreversible damage to the lungs.

Emphysema often occurs in people who also have bronchitis, which is a condition that makes bronchiole walls inflamed and covered with more mucus than normal. Together, these two conditions are called chronic obstructive pulmonary disease (COPD).

Asthma

Asthma is a condition in which the muscles lining the terminal bronchioles constrict. The lining also over-produces mucus. Both of these responses narrow the airway, making it particularly difficult to breathe out. The narrow airway produces a wheezing sound during exhaling. In asthmatics, an attack is brought on by an environmental trigger such as stress or cold air, although it is usually triggered by an allergen such as house dust or animal fur. Asthma affects lung function because it reduces air flow. It does not damage alveoli and so there is no reduction in surface area.

3 Organisms exchange substances with their environment

Example

Graphs and patterns

Study the graph, which shows the change in the number of asthma patients and four common air pollutants over a 20-year period. The air pollutants are particle matter, sulfur dioxide, nitrogen oxide and carbon monoxide.

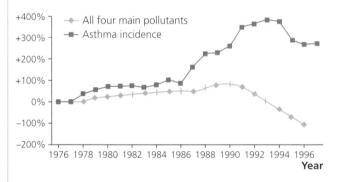

(a) Describe the pattern of incidence of asthma. [3]

(b) Evaluate the claim that air pollution causes asthma. [3]

Answer

You have to match up your answer to the number of marks. If the graph is one straight line, there will usually be 1 mark for writing something like 'as X increases, Y increases'. However, for a more complex graph like the one here, there will often be 2 or 3 marks available.

(a) There is a slow increase up to 1986. There is a rapid increase from 1986 to 1993. There is a fall after the peak in 1993.

(b) There is a correlation between the number of pollutants and the incidence of asthma. However, a correlation does not mean a cause. Something else could be causing the increase, such as more allergens.

Exam tip

There will always be questions about data in the exam. Tables and graphs are nothing to be afraid of. In fact, they are often easy marks as the information is there for you.

Exam tip

Part (a) asks you to 'describe', so there is no need to explain anything here. Part (b) asks you to 'evaluate', which means to look at both sides.

Now test yourself

TESTED

6 Explain the difference between the terms *respiration* and *breathing*.

7 List three ways in which the lungs are adapted to speed up the process of diffusion.

8 Explain why people with emphysema often get breathless when they do anything strenuous.

Answers on p. 109

Digestion and absorption

The digestive system

The intestine (or gut) is a long tube that passes through the middle of the body (Figure 3.10). Food goes in the mouth and is digested so that it can be absorbed into the blood. Anything that cannot be digested cannot be absorbed and so passes straight through. The content of the gut is not part of your body. It is a mixture of partially digested food, cells from the gut lining, digestive enzymes and bacteria.

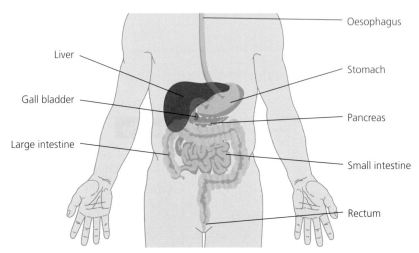

Figure 3.10 The human digestive system

The molecules in our food are needed to build and maintain our bodies. The three key groups of organic molecules are carbohydrates, lipids and proteins. The food we eat consists of a complex mixture of these three types, together with simpler ones such as water, vitamins and salts.

Digestion involves breaking down these large molecules so that they are simple, soluble and can be absorbed into the blood. **Large biological molecules** are **hydrolysed** by enzymes to produce **smaller molecules** that can be absorbed across **cell membranes**. Once inside the body, smaller molecules are built up into large ones by condensation.

> **Exam tip**
>
> Condensation and hydrolysis are common themes for exam questions. Make sure you get them the right way round. Condensation reactions *produce* water, whereas hydrolysis reactions *use* water.

Now test yourself

9 Explain the difference between condensation and hydrolysis reactions.

Answers on p. 109

Digestion

Carbohydrate digestion

Carbohydrate digestion begins in the mouth. Saliva contains the enzyme **salivary amylase**, which hydrolyses starch into maltose. This digestion is not really significant because:
- we generally swallow food before the enzyme has a chance to work
- hot food can denature the enzyme
- some people do not make salivary amylase — it is genetic

There is no carbohydrate digestion in the stomach. The acidic pH in the stomach stops the salivary amylase from working and the stomach enzymes digest only protein.

The main region for carbohydrate digestion is the small intestine. Food leaving the stomach and entering the small intestine has two digestive juices added to it: pancreatic juice from the pancreas and bile from the liver. Bile has no part in carbohydrate digestion but pancreatic juice is vital.

1 Starch is digested by **pancreatic amylase** in pancreatic juice. This produces maltose, which joins lactose and sucrose already in the gut. So there are three disaccharides that need digesting.

2 The disaccharides are hydrolysed into monosaccharides by **maltase**, **sucrase** and **lactase**. These enzymes are fixed in the membranes of the intestinal epithelial cells (Figure 3.11). The monosaccharides can then be absorbed.

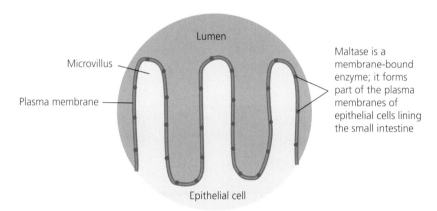

Figure 3.11 The location of the maltase enzymes in the wall of the intestine

Now test yourself

TESTED ☐

10 Where are the enzymes that break down maltose located?
11 Name the main region of the gut where carbohydrate digestion takes place.
12 Why is it an advantage to have enzymes fixed in the wall of the intestine rather than having them free in the lumen?

Answers on p. 109

Lipid digestion

Lipids and water do not mix and so any lipids eaten tend to reach the small intestine in globule/droplet form. **Lipid digestion** is a two-part process:

1 Physical digestion. **Bile salts** in bile lower the surface tension between lipids and water so that large droplets are split into many smaller ones. This process is celled **emulsification** and it greatly increases the surface area of the lipid droplets.

2 Chemical digestion. The enzyme **lipase**, secreted in pancreatic juice, hydrolyses triglycerides into fatty acids and glycerol.

The end result of these processes is a mixture of glycerol, fatty acids and monoglycerides (glycerol attached to one fatty acid). The bile salts form **micelles**, which are tiny droplets (4–8 nm across) that contain the products of lipid digestion on their surface. Micelles are constantly ferrying the components of lipid digestion from the lumen to the epithelial cells so that they can be absorbed.

Now test yourself

13 Lipase enzymes are water soluble, so they only work on the surface of lipid droplets. Use this information to explain why bile salts are so important.

Answers on p. 109

Protein digestion

Protein digestion takes place in both the stomach and the small intestine. There are several different **protease** enzymes, also called **proteolytic** enzymes, but they all work by hydrolysing peptide bonds. They can be roughly divided into three types:

- **endopeptidases**, which cut within the protein, turning long chains of polypeptides into shorter chains
- **exopeptidases**, which remove the terminal (end) amino acids from polypeptide chains
- **dipeptidases**, which are membrane-bound enzymes similar to the enzymes that digest disaccharides. They hydrolyse dipeptides into individual amino acids

It is important to appreciate that these enzymes combine to be far more effective than each single type would be on its own. For example, endopeptidase enzymes make more 'ends' for the exopeptidase enzymes to work on.

Absorption

Adaptations of the ileum

The mammalian **ileum** (the main part of the small intestine) is adapted to absorb the products of digestion as follows (Figure 3.12):

- It is long.
- Its lining is folded into millions of projections called villi.
- The epithelial cells covering the villi are themselves folded into many microvilli.

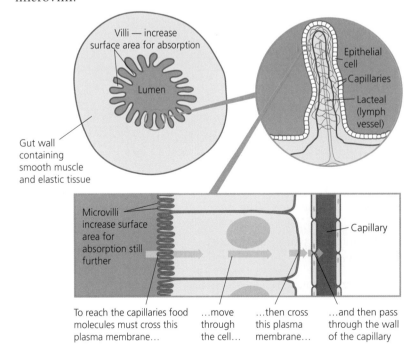

Figure 3.12 How digested food molecules reach the capillaries in the gut wall

The above adaptations all combine to create a massive surface area of membrane in direct contact with the gut contents. There are lots of digestive enzymes and transport proteins embedded in the membrane. In addition:

- the epithelial cells themselves are thin, creating a short diffusing pathway
- the epithelial cells have many mitochondria, to synthesise ATP for active transport
- there is an efficient blood supply running through all the villi, so that substances are transported away as soon as they are absorbed. This speeds up absorption by maintaining a diffusion gradient

Amino acids

Amino acids are absorbed by a process known as **co-transport**. The membranes of the epithelial cells contain several different amino acid transporters, which absorb the different types of amino acid such as acidic, basic or neutral. They all transport amino acids only after binding with sodium. Once a symport protein is loaded up with both an amino acid and sodium, it undergoes a shape change that transports both molecules to the other side before going back to its original shape. The whole process is dependent on the concentration gradient of sodium. If there is no sodium gradient, there is no amino acid absorption.

Monosaccharides

Once the digestive enzymes have converted all the carbohydrates in the diet, the resulting **monosaccharides** need to be absorbed. By far the most common monosaccharide is glucose, which (like amino acids) is absorbed by co-transport. It involves both facilitated diffusion and active transport, and absorbs sodium ions (Na^+) at the same time. See p. 44 for more details on the absorption of glucose.

See p. 44 for more details on the absorption of glucose.

> **Exam tip**
>
> You are expected to know the cellular and molecular details of absorption. Make sure you can explain how the fine structure of an intestinal epithelial cell adapts it for the absorption of digested food.

Now test yourself

TESTED ☐

14 The absorption of amino acids, glucose and sodium also causes the absorption of water from the gut. Explain how.

Answers on p. 109

Answers on p. 109

Lipids

The absorption of lipids is a two-stage process:

1 The epithelial cells absorb the fatty acids, glycerol and monoglycerides because they can pass easily through the lipid part of the membrane. The micelles are not absorbed. Once inside the cell, all the components of lipid digestion pass to the endoplasmic reticulum there they are recombined into triglycerides. They are then packaged into **chylomicrons**, which contain, in order of abundance, triglycerides, phospholipids, cholesterol and protein. The chylomicrons are released from the epithelial cells by exocytosis.

2 The chylomicrons pass into the lacteals, which are lymph capillaries. There is one in the centre of each villus. From here, the chylomicrons are carried in the lymphatic system, finally joining the blood system in the subclavian vein, which is in the chest cavity, just under the collar bone. From here the chylomicrons are distributed around the rest of the body. Lipids are insoluble in water and so chylomicrons are the main method of lipid transport in the blood.

> **Exam tip**
>
> Whenever you are about to write the word *digested*, think about using *hydrolysed* instead. It makes examiners happy.

Mass transport in animals

When multicellular organisms develop organs of exchange such as lungs, guts and gills, they need a transport system to move substances over large distances because diffusion is simply too slow. Most transport systems consist of a series of tubes in which an efficient supply of materials is moved around under pressure. These systems are called **mass transport** systems. Plants have xylem and phloem, whereas vertebrates have a blood system.

Haemoglobin

REVISED

Red blood cells are unique cells that carry oxygen. They also, indirectly, help to carry carbon dioxide. The scientific name for red blood cells is erythrocytes, which just means 'red cells'. They are made in the bone marrow and are bi-convex in shape, which allows them to carry a useful amount of oxygen but to load and unload it quickly (Figure 3.13).

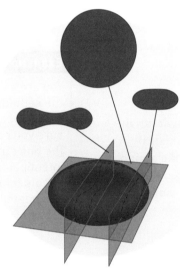

Figure 3.13 Red cells are bi-convex in shape, which is a perfect compromise between the maximum volume of a sphere and the maximum surface area of a flat disc

Now test yourself

TESTED

15 Red blood cells have no nucleus. Suggest why this is an advantage.

Answers on p. 109

Haemoglobin is a complex **protein** with a **quaternary structure**. It consists of four polypeptide chains (**globins**) attached to four iron-containing parts (**haems**) (Figure 3.14). At the centre of each haem is an Fe^{2+} ion that attaches to an oxygen molecule (O_2). As a chemical equation:

$$Hb + 4O_2 \rightleftharpoons HbO_8$$

Each haemoglobin molecule can combine with four oxygen molecules to form bright-red **oxyhaemoglobin**. The clever thing about haemoglobin is the cooperative nature of oxygen binding. When the first oxygen molecule combines with a haem group, the shape of the molecule changes so that it becomes easier for the other oxygen molecules to bind.

Exam practice answers and quick quizzes at www.hoddereducation.co.uk/myrevisionnotes

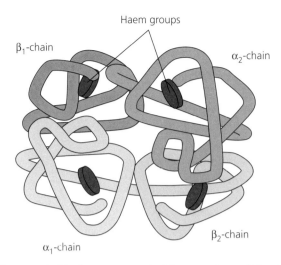

β₁-chain

Haem groups

α₂-chain

α₁-chain

β₂-chain

Figure 3.14 Haemoglobin is composed of four polypeptide chains, each attached to a haem group

The oxyhaemoglobin dissociation curve

The key property of haemoglobin is that it combines with oxygen where it is abundant, but then releases it again where it is scarce. This property is shown by a graph called the **oxyhaemoglobin dissociation curve** (Figure 3.15). This graph is a favourite topic of examiners, but candidates often find it difficult.

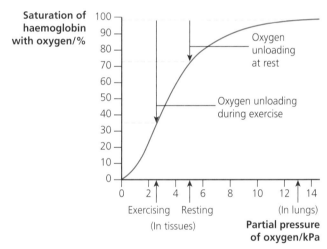

Figure 3.15 The oxyhaemoglobin dissociation curve of human haemoglobin

On the x-axis, the term *partial pressure* is a bit of physics. For our purposes, it means 'how much oxygen is available'. The y-axis is more straightforward. It means 'how many haemoglobin molecules are carrying oxygen?' A value of 80% means that 80% of haemoglobin molecules are carrying oxygen and 20% are not.

So the graph simply shows that haemoglobin will pick up oxygen where it is abundant (the lungs), but it will release oxygen when it is scarce (the respiring tissues in the rest of the body). To do this, haemoglobin must be able to change its affinity for (attraction to) oxygen.

At the lungs, haemoglobin becomes almost fully saturated with oxygen — about 98% is a normal value. Oxygenated blood is then transported to the respiring tissues all around the body. What makes haemoglobin give up its oxygen? When a red blood cell enters a capillary, it begins to unload its oxygen:

1 The respiring cells make carbon dioxide, which diffuses into the blood and into the red cell.

2 The enzyme carbonic anhydrase catalyses the reaction:

$$H_2O + CO_2 \rightleftharpoons H_2CO_3 \rightleftharpoons H^+ + HCO_3^-$$

This simply means that water combines with carbon dioxide to make carbonic acid. Like all acids, carbonic acid splits to form hydrogen ions and hydrogen carbonate ions. Hydrogen ions are what make solutions acidic.

3 Vitally, the H^+ ions lower the affinity of haemoglobin for oxygen. So haemoglobin releases some of its oxygen molecules.

4 The oxygen molecules are free to diffuse into the cells.

5 The remaining HCO_3^- ions diffuse into the plasma, leaving the red blood cell with a slightly positive charge. To balance this out, chloride ions (Cl^-) diffuse from the plasma into the red blood cell.

Therefore, the higher the **carbon dioxide concentration**, the lower the affinity of haemoglobin for oxygen. It is a really clever mechanism: the faster the cells and tissues are respiring, the faster the oxygen is delivered. If the muscles are working really hard, there will be more carbon dioxide and more H^+ ions, so the affinity of haemoglobin for oxygen is lowered and so more oxygen is released. This is known as **the Bohr effect**. It results in the oxyhaemoglobin dissociation curve moving to the right. The higher the concentration of carbon dioxide, the more the curve shifts to the right, showing that haemoglobin has a lower affinity for oxygen (Figure 3.16).

> **The Bohr effect** is the shift to the right of the position of the oxyhaemoglobin dissociation curve in the presence of extra carbon dioxide.

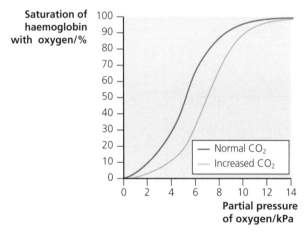

Figure 3.16 The Bohr effect

> **Exam tip**
>
> In questions about haemoglobin, try to use words like *affinity*, *saturation* and *partial pressure*.

Now test yourself

TESTED

16 Explain why red blood cells need the enzyme carbonic anhydrase.

17 Why is it not correct to say that haemoglobin has a high affinity for oxygen?

Answers on p. 109

Haemoglobin in other organisms

There are several examples of different types of haemoglobin in invertebrates. Most do not have a complex circulatory system, nor do they have what we would recognise as blood, but some have haemoglobin in their body tissues. Examples include:

- tubifex worms, which are related to earthworms — they are often called sewer worms and survive in oxygen-poor water
- bloodworms, which are the larvae of a type of midge, often found in ponds and lakes

The key point is that their haemoglobin has a high affinity for oxygen and it can become saturated with oxygen even at low partial pressures. This gives them an advantage: they can respire and survive in conditions of low oxygen that would prove lethal to many other species.

The blood system

The **blood circulation** in a **mammal** is closed, meaning that the blood circulates in a complete circuit — it never leaves the **blood vessels**. The sight of blood is a sure sign that a blood vessel has broken. Substances can pass in and out of the blood through capillary walls, but blood stays in blood vessels.

Humans and other mammals have a double circulatory system in which blood flows through the heart twice for each circuit around the body (Figure 3.17):

- the pulmonary circulation takes blood to the lungs to take up oxygen
- the systemic circulation takes the oxygenated blood around the body to the tissues

body → heart → lungs → heart → body

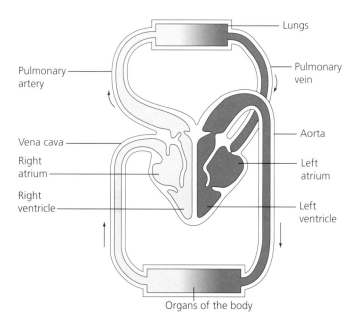

Figure 3.17 The human double circulatory system

We need two circulatory systems because, when the blood goes to the lungs, it takes up oxygen *but loses pressure*. The blood must therefore return to the heart for a boost. It needs to gain enough pressure to allow it to travel around the whole body.

Blood vessels

You need to know about four types of blood vessels: arteries, arterioles, veins and capillaries.

The walls of blood vessels have three layers (Figure 3.18):
- the outer layer — the tough **tunica externa**
- the middle layer — the **tunica media**
- the inner layer — the **endothelium**

It is the difference in the middle layer that gives blood vessels their different properties. Capillaries, however, do not have a middle layer, just a one-cell thick endothelium.

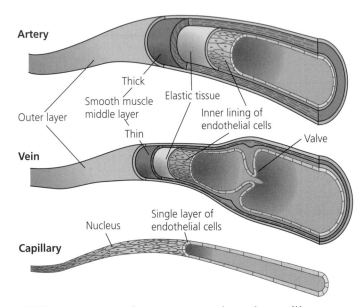

Figure 3.18 The structure of an artery, a vein and a capillary

Arteries

Arteries are adapted to withstand pressure. When the heart beats, the left ventricle forces blood into the body's largest artery, the **aorta**. From here, blood enters the major arteries of the body, leading to all the major organs and limbs. The middle layers of the artery walls are rich in muscle and, vitally, **elastic fibres**. This gives them powerful recoil properties so they can withstand the pressure surge of each heartbeat.

Arterioles

Arterioles are adapted to control blood flow. By the time blood reaches the arterioles, it has lost much of its pressure because it has been absorbed by artery walls. The walls of the arterioles do not need as many elastic fibres, but they do have a lot of circular muscle fibres. This means that arterioles are capable of either:
- vasoconstriction — they get smaller when the circular muscles contract
- vasodilation — they get larger when the circular muscles relax

In this way, blood flow to certain areas of the body can be controlled. For example, vasodilation causes the skin to redden, whereas vasoconstriction causes it to go pale. Viagra makes certain arterioles dilate too.

Exam tip

Muscles *contract*, vessels *constrict*. Don't get them mixed up.

Veins

Veins are adapted to increase blood flow when pressure is low. Compared with arteries, veins have a larger lumen and a thinner wall. This minimises friction so blood can flow more easily. The walls are made of tough connective tissue and there are fewer elastic or muscle fibres. Veins also have valves that can close to prevent backflow.

Capillaries

Capillaries allow exchange between blood and cells. They are the smallest blood vessels and they do not function on their own. Instead, they form a **capillary bed** — an interweaving network of capillaries supplying organs and tissues. Capillary walls (the endothelium) are just one cell thick. The function of capillaries is to allow metabolic exchange of materials between blood and tissue fluid. All living cells in the body are surrounded by tissue fluid.

> A **capillary bed** is a network of capillaries that supply blood to a specific organ or area of the body.

TESTED ☐

Now test yourself

18 Name the blood vessels that supply blood to:
  (a) the heart muscle
  (b) the lungs
  (c) the kidneys
19 Explain how the walls of capillaries are adapted to their function.

Answers on p. 109

Tissue fluid

Cells absorb oxygen and nutrients from **tissue fluid**, exchanging them for carbon dioxide, waste products and any substances that the cell makes, such as hormones. It is the function of the circulatory system to keep the composition of tissue fluid as constant as possible. Tissue fluid is basically blood plasma without the cells and large proteins, which are too large to leave the blood.

Two forces are involved in the formation and drainage of tissue fluid (Figure 3.19):
● hydrostatic pressure — the physical pressure of the blood, created by the heart, which forces fluid out of the blood
● water potential — the pressure exerted by dissolved substances in a fluid, which draws water back into the blood

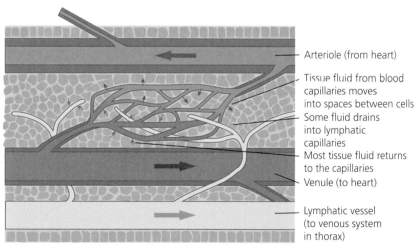

Figure 3.19 The circulation of tissue fluid and the formation of lymph

At the arterial end of a capillary, the hydrostatic pressure is greater than the water potential so that tissue fluid is forced out of the blood. As blood flows along the capillary, it loses volume and therefore loses hydrostatic pressure. However, the proteins that cannot leave the blood exert an osmotic force. So, at the venous end of the capillary, the water potential becomes greater than the hydrostatic pressure and so water is drawn back into the blood (Figure 3.20).

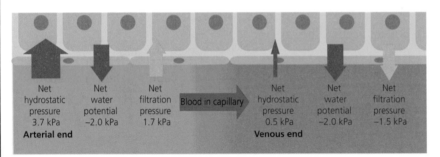

| Net hydrostatic pressure 3.7 kPa | Net water potential −2.0 kPa | Net filtration pressure 1.7 kPa | Blood in capillary | Net hydrostatic pressure 0.5 kPa | Net water potential −2.0 kPa | Net filtration pressure −1.5 kPa |

Arterial end   Venous end

Figure 3.20 As blood flows along a capillary, it loses pressure. When the water potential becomes greater than the hydrostatic pressure, fluid begins to return to the blood

Now test yourself

TESTED

20 Name three substances that will pass from blood into tissue fluid.

Answers on p. 109

Lymph vessels

Lymph vessels also drain tissue fluid. The arterioles deliver 100% of the fluid that reaches the tissues, but the veins only take about 99.9% of it back. The remaining tissue fluid passes into lymph vessels that begin in the tissues themselves, so think of lymph vessels as an extra set of veins.

Some tissue fluid, together with some molecules that are too large to pass into the blood, pass into the lymph system. This fluid drains into progressively larger vessels until it drains back into the blood high in the chest cavity, just under the collar bone. This lymphatic drainage is small but vital. If the lymph vessels become blocked — by parasites, for example — the affected area swells up as tissue fluid accumulates. This is known as **elephantiasis**.

Heart structure and function

REVISED

The human heart is a muscular organ with one simple function: to create blood pressure. The heart has four chambers: two **atria** and two **ventricles** (Figure 3.21). The atria are simply there to load the ventricles with the right amount of blood. When full, the ventricles contract powerfully to create the pressure that forces blood into arteries. Contraction of heart muscle is known as **systole** and relaxation is known as **diastole**.

To understand how the heart works, it is important to remember cause and effect. The heart muscle is stimulated to contract, which changes the pressure in the chambers. Blood always flows from areas of high pressure to areas of lower pressure. It is this flow of blood that causes the opening and closing of the valves.

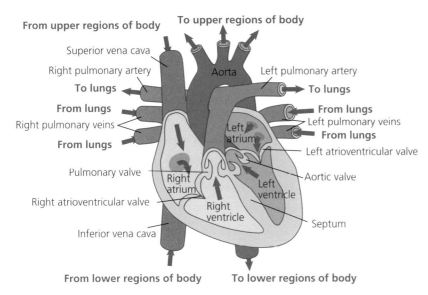

Figure 3.21 The structure of the human heart

Pressure and volume changes during the cardiac cycle

The **cardiac cycle** is the sequence of events involved in one heart beat (Figure 3.22). If your pulse rate is 70, your heart is going through the cardiac cycle 70 times per minute.

The **cardiac cycle** is the series of events in one heart beat.

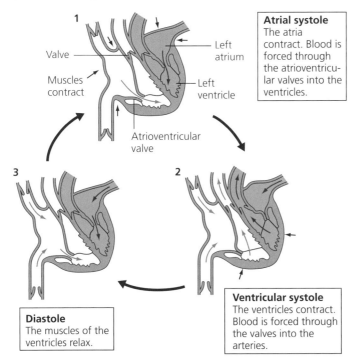

Atrial systole
The atria contract. Blood is forced through the atrioventricular valves into the ventricles.

Ventricular systole
The ventricles contract. Blood is forced through the valves into the arteries.

Diastole
The muscles of the ventricles relax.

Figure 3.22 The three key stages of the cardiac cycle

The pressure and volume changes and associated valve movements during the cardiac cycle are summarised as follows:

atria fill → atria contract → atrioventricular valves open → ventricles fill → ventricles contract → atrioventricular valves shut → pressure rises dramatically → semilunar valves open → aorta and pulmonary artery fill → as soon as the pressure begins to drop, semilunar valves shut → atria and ventricles relax → heart begin to fill with blood → cycle repeats itself

Exam tip

You should be able to tell the stage of the cardiac cycle by looking at the valves — which are open and which are closed?

3 Organisms exchange substances with their environment

AQA AS/A-level Year 1 Biology   73

Now test yourself

21 Put these events of the cardiac cycle in order.
 A Semilunar valves shut
 B Semilunar valves open
 C Atrioventricular valves shut
 D Atrioventricular valves open
22 Is there ever a time in the cardiac cycle when all of the valves are open at the same time? Explain your answer.
23 If the semilunar valves are shut, which chambers are contracting?
24 Which chamber of the heart is responsible for creating blood pressure?

Answers on p. 109

Understanding the cardiac cycle is all about pressure changes and valves. Figure 3.23 shows the pressure changes in one heart beat. There are three lines: the left atrium, the left ventricle and the aorta. Even if there were no labels, you could tell which was which because:

● the pressure in the atria is always low, so it is the bottom line
● the pressure in the aorta (the body's biggest artery) is always high, so it is the top line
● the pressure in the ventricles varies dramatically, so it is the line that rises and falls rapidly

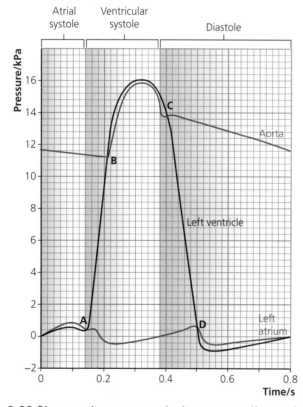

Figure 3.23 Changes in pressure during one cardiac cycle

Now test yourself

25 Study Figure 3.23.
 (a) Between which two points is the aorta filling with blood?
 (b) The graph shows the pressure changes in the left side of the heart. Suggest how the graph would be different for the right side.

Answers on p. 109

The conducting pathway of the heart

Heart muscle is myogenic — it is a remarkable tissue that contracts on its own, without nerve impulses from the brain. However, all the cells need to contract at the right time otherwise the heart cannot pump effectively. The chambers should contract only when they are full of blood, so the heart has a conducting pathway of specialised muscle fibres to ensure the right sequence of events (Figure 3.24). The atria must contract first and then, when full, the ventricles follow. This means a delay is needed to allow the ventricles to fill. The full sequence is as follows:

● The heart beat is initiated by a group of cells called the **sinoatrial node (SAN)** near the top of the right atrium.
● These cells produce waves of electrical activity, similar to nerve impulses.
● The impulse spreads over the atria, which then contract.
● A tough band of connective tissue prevents the impulse spreading to the ventricles.
● The impulse is picked up by the **atrioventricular node (AVN)** which, after a short delay, passes the impulse down the middle of the ventricles in the **bundle of His** — a specialised bunch of muscle fibres that transmits the impulse without causing contraction.
● At the apex of the heart (the bottom of the ventricles) the impulses reach the **Purkinje fibres**. These cause contraction of the thick ventricle muscle, starting at the apex so that blood is forced upwards through the semilunar valves.

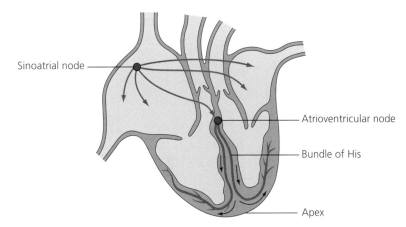

Figure 3.24 The route of electrical activity that makes the heart beat in a smooth sequence

Now test yourself

26 Explain what is meant by the term *myogenic*.
27 Explain why it is important that there is a slight delay after the atria contract.

Answers on p. 109

Cardiac output

The volume of blood pumped with each heart beat is called the **stroke volume**. A typical value is around $80\,cm^3$. This means that each time the heart beats, $80\,cm^3$ of blood is sent to the lungs via the pulmonary artery and $80\,cm^3$ is sent to the rest of the body. All of the chambers of the heart have the same volume.

TESTED

The total amount of blood pumped per minute is known as the **cardiac output**. It is calculated as using this formula:

cardiac output = stroke volume × heart rate

Therefore, the cardiac output for a person at rest might be $80\,cm^3 \times 70$ beats per minute = $5600\,cm^3$, or 5.6 litres.

Now test yourself

28 If an athlete has a stroke volume of $100\,cm^3$ and a heart rate of 160 bpm, work out his cardiac output.

Answer on p. 110

Cardiovascular disease

Cardiovascular disease starts with a build-up of fatty material inside the walls of blood vessels. This may go on for years with no symptoms, but if the arteries get narrower and narrower, a time will come when not enough blood can get through.

Atheroma

Atheroma is fatty material that builds up in the walls of arteries, causing them to get narrower (Figure 3.25). It also causes the artery lining (the endothelium) to get rougher. **Atherosclerosis** is the process of atheroma developing inside the artery walls.

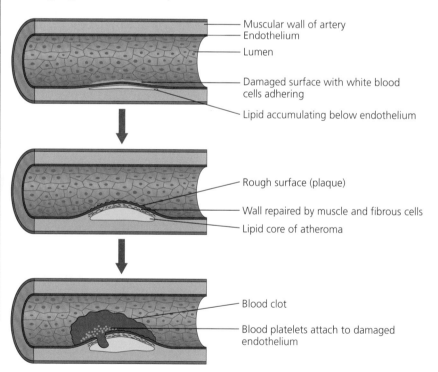

Figure 3.25 The development of atheroma

Thrombosis and aneurysm

Arteries have to cope with high blood pressure so their walls have to be relatively thick and elastic. The walls of arteries have several layers. The endothelium of a healthy artery should be smooth and unbroken.

Over time, fatty deposits begin to develop under the endothelium. This makes the endothelium rough and sticky, and narrows the lumen. If the

> **Typical mistake**
>
> Candidates often state that atheroma builds up in the lumen or the artery, implying that the fatty material covers the endothelium. In fact, the fatty deposit accumulates within the artery wall, so that the endothelium is pushed inwards.

> **Exam tip**
>
> Candidates often get bogged down trying to give the exact components of atheroma, but that level of detail is not required in the specification.

fatty material breaks through the endothelium, it can lead to a blood clot known as a **thrombosis**, which can block the artery. A stroke is caused by a blood clot or burst blood vessel in the brain, so that an area of the brain cells die. The symptoms depend on the size of the damaged area and its precise location in the brain.

An **aneurysm** is a ballooning of the artery that results from a weakness in the vessel wall coupled with high blood pressure (Figure 3.26). The endothelium and middle layer (tunica media) of the artery split so that just the outer layer (tunica externa) is left intact. This is a serious medical crisis that needs surgery. A burst aneurysm will quickly be fatal due massive internal bleeding.

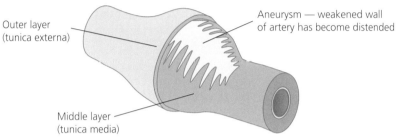

Outer layer (tunica externa)

Aneurysm — weakened wall of artery has become distended

Middle layer (tunica media)

Figure 3.26 An aneurysm

Myocardial infarction

A blocked coronary artery causes a myocardial infarction or heart attack (Figure 3.27). It is caused by an interruption in the blood flow to the heart muscle, so the cells immediately run short of oxygen, cannot respire and therefore die. The symptoms include severe pain in the chest and upper body, particularly on the left side, sweating and shortness of breath. The heart can recover from a small amount of muscle death, but large areas can cause complete heart failure, which is almost always fatal.

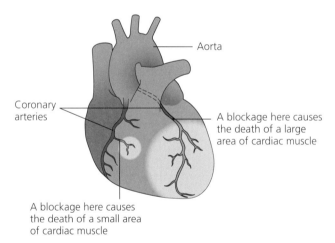

Aorta

Coronary arteries

A blockage here causes the death of a large area of cardiac muscle

A blockage here causes the death of a small area of cardiac muscle

Figure 3.27 A blockage in a coronary artery can cause the death of an area of heart muscle

Risk factors associated with coronary heart disease

Some people are predisposed to develop **coronary heart disease (CHD)**, meaning that they have inherited genes that increase the risk. Lifestyle factors also contribute. These are the main risk factors in the development of CHD.

● Diet — too much saturated fat appears to speed up the development of atheroma. Animal tissue such as eggs, cheese, cream and red meat tends to be high in saturated fats.

> **Exam tip**
>
> Candidates often lose marks by missing out details they know. An answer such as 'The heart muscles cells are starved of blood and so they die' would be much better expressed as 'The heart muscle cells are starved of oxygen, so cannot respire and therefore die'.

- Blood cholesterol — animal fat is also high in cholesterol, which is a major constituent of atheroma.
- Cigarette smoking — there are lots of different substances in cigarette smoke, including nicotine and carbon monoxide. Some of them make the arteries constrict. This reduces blood flow and increases blood pressure. Carbon monoxide binds to haemoglobin and prevents it carrying oxygen. If 20% of your haemoglobin is not working, your heart will have to pump 20% more blood to make up the difference.
- High blood pressure — this is the pressure created in arteries when the heart beats, and it varies according to the strength of the beat and the size and condition of the arteries. High blood pressure can damage artery walls, increasing the risk of atheroma. It also increases the risk of aneurysm and stroke.

> **Coronary heart disease (CHD)** refers to a build-up of atheroma in the coronary arteries that supply the heart muscle with blood.

These are additional risk factors:
- Exercise — having a sedentary lifestyle can increase the chances of developing CHD.
- Weight — a person's weight is usually measured as body mass index (BMI), which is calculated as follows:

$$BMI = \frac{mass\ (kg)}{height^2\ (m^2)}$$

Someone with a BMI of over 25 is classed as overweight, while over 30 they are obese. Obesity brings a whole range of health problems that include CHD as well as type 2 diabetes and joint pain.
- Age — the older we get, the more our lifestyle has a chance to take its toll. Our tissues also get less elastic. Arteries lose their elasticity and are more likely to tear or split as a result of high blood pressure.

In the UK, over 25% of deaths each year are directly due to CHD, making it the biggest killer and pushing cancer into second place.

Now test yourself

TESTED

29 A person is 1.56 m tall and weighs 94 kg. Are they obese? Explain your answer.

Answer on p. 110

Mass transport in plants

Xylem

REVISED

Xylem is a specialised conducting tissue that transports water and dissolved ions up the stem from the roots towards the leaves (Figure 3.28). This example of mass transport is known as the **transpiration stream**. The loss of water vapour from the upper surface of a plant is known as **transpiration**. The vast majority of this water is lost from the stomata, most of which are on the underside of leaves.

> The **transpiration stream** is the movement of water and minerals through the plant in the xylem tissue, from the roots to the leaves.
>
> **Transpiration** is the loss of water vapour from the upper surfaces of a plant.

Xylem vessels develop when cells elongate and then die, so that their contents are lost. Their cell walls become strengthened with extra **cellulose** and a waterproof material called **lignin**. Many xylem vessels join end to end so that a continuous pathway is formed from the root up to the leaves.

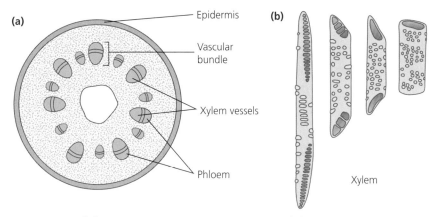

Figure 3.28 (a) A cross-section of a plant root. (b) Xylem vessels

The movement of water up a plant

Leaves must be organs of gas exchange in order for photosynthesis to take place. Carbon dioxide needs to diffuse in and oxygen needs to diffuse out. To allow efficient gas exchange, leaves have stomata and loosely packed mesophyll cells. As a consequence, a large surface area of cells in the leaf is exposed to the atmosphere and there is rapid water loss by evaporation (Figure 3.29). The force that draws water up the plant in the xylem is described below.

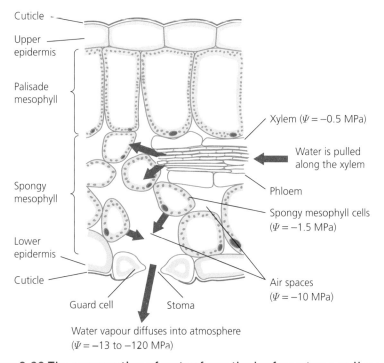

Figure 3.29 The evaporation of water from the leaf creates a pull on the xylem

The cohesion-tension theory

The water potential of dry air is very low. This causes evaporation and is one of the basic forces that drives that water cycle.

1 Water evaporates from the wet cell walls inside leaves and passes out through the stomata.
2 The loss of water creates a pull on the xylem.

3 Water molecules are cohesive (the molecules attract one another). They form a continuous column from the leaves right down to the roots, which can withstand great tension.

4 Therefore, evaporation from the leaves creates a pull that draws water up to the top of the plant.

This is the **cohesion-tension theory**.

Factors that affect the speed of transpiration

Transpiration happens by evaporation, so the conditions that speed up the process are:

● Dry air — the dryer the air, the lower the water potential. This means there is a greater **water potential gradient** between the air inside and outside of the leaf. When air is humid, the water potential gradient is smaller and evaporation is slower.

● Warmth — heat increases the kinetic energy of the water molecules, so they evaporate more quickly.

● Wind — in still conditions, pockets of humid air develop around the stomata. These are called diffusion shells. Wind blows away the diffusion shells. This increases the water potential gradient between air and leaf, so when it is windy evaporation is greater.

Measuring transpiration

The **potometer** is a simple piece of apparatus that measures transpiration — think of it as a transparent extension of the xylem (Figure 3.30). The plant transpires, which draws water up the xylem. In turn, this causes the bubble to move towards the plant, showing how much water is being lost.

The rate of transpiration is measured as the volume of water per unit leaf area per unit time — for example, $3.2\,\mathrm{cm^3\,cm^{-2}\,min^{-1}}$. Without leaf area and time, you cannot have meaningful comparisons between different plants, species or conditions.

> **Exam tip**
>
> In questions about practical procedures, examiners often ask candidates to suggest suitable units. However, they sometimes lose marks by forgetting to include 'per unit time'.

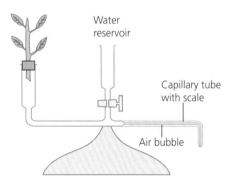

Figure 3.30 A potometer

> **Now test yourself**
>
> TESTED ☐
>
> **30** What is the difference between transpiration and the transpiration stream?
>
> **Answers on p. 110**

Phloem and translocation

REVISED ☐

Translocation is the movement of sugars (mainly sucrose) and other organic molecules around the plant in the **phloem**. There are two important words here:

● **Source** — the part of the plan where the sugar molecules originate. This can be either a photosynthesising leaf making new sugars or storage organs releasing sugars that were made earlier.

● **Sink** — the part of the plant where the sugar molecules are going to. Often this is the roots, leaves, fruits or growing points (meristems — sites of mitosis).

> **Translocation** is the movement of organic molecules (mainly sucrose) around the plant from source to sink in the phloem.

Like xylem, phloem vessels are elongated cells that join end to end to form long continuous tubes (Figure 3.31). There are two basic types of phloem cells: sieve tubes, which actually transport the fluids, and companion cells, which control the activities of the sieve tubes and keep them alive. The differences between xylem and phloem are:

● Phloem vessels are not dead — they contain living cytoplasm. The sieve tubes have a greatly reduced number of organelles and these are concentrated close to the cell wall so as not to impede the flow. The companion cells have a full set of organelles, including nuclei. Xylem vessels have no organelles at all, just walls.
● Phloem vessels move substances in all directions around a plant, whereas xylem vessels just move substances up towards the leaves.
● Phloem vessels contain dissolved organic substances, the majority of which are sugars made by photosynthesis. Xylem vessels just transport water and dissolved ions.
● Movement in phloem is caused by positive hydrostatic pressure, whereas movement in xylem is driven by negative pressure. If you pierced a phloem vessel with a pin, fluid would be forced out. If you pierced a xylem vessel, air would be drawn in.

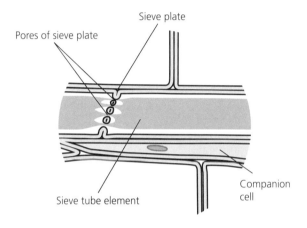

Figure 3.31 Phloem tissue

Now test yourself

TESTED

31 What is the difference between translocation and transpiration?

Answers on p. 110

The evidence for translocation

We know that the sugars found in various parts of the plant have originated in the sources and been transported in the phloem. The evidence for this includes **tracers** and **ringing experiments**.

Tracing radioactive ^{14}C

If you provide a plant with carbon dioxide in which the carbon atom is the radioactive isotope ^{14}C, you can follow its progress around the plant using a process called autoradiography. Initially, the ^{14}C is found in the leaves, first in glucose and then starch. Then it can be traced to the phloem, where it is often in sucrose — the most common transport sugar in plants. Finally, the radioactivity can be found in the sinks, often as starch. This is very strong evidence that the phloem is responsible for transporting the products of photosynthesis around the plant.

Ringing experiments

In most trees, the phloem vessels are found on the inside of the bark, whereas functioning xylem vessels are found in the outer part of the wood, just under the bark. If you remove a ring of bark around the circumference of a tree, you remove the phloem. When this is done, sugars accumulate in the phloem above the ring, suggesting that phloem is moving sugars down the plant from the leaves to the roots.

The mechanism of translocation

The **mass flow hypothesis** is the current favoured explanation for the mechanism of translocation:

1 In the sources, sugars are actively transported into the phloem.
2 This lowers the water potential in the phloem.
3 So water enters the phloem by osmosis, increasing the hydrostatic pressure.
4 At the sinks, sugar is actively transported out of the phloem.
5 This raises the water potential in the phloem, so water follows the solute, into the cells of the sink, by osmosis.
6 This lowers the hydrostatic pressure in the phloem in that region.
7 Overall, fluid is forced from the areas of high hydrostatic pressure to the areas of low hydrostatic pressure.

> **Typical mistake**
>
> To avoid confusing xylem and phloem, remember your Fs: *food flows in phloem*. Don't write that in the exam.

Exam practice

1 The graphs show a spirometer trace of the pressure and volume changes in the lungs during one breathing cycle.

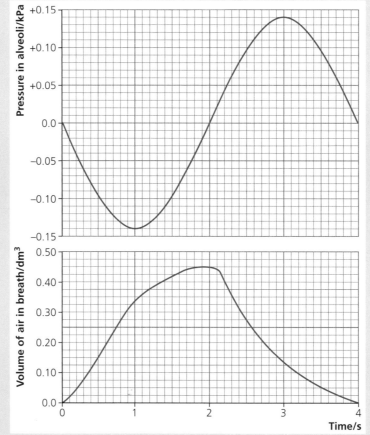

(a) During which time is the person:
  (i) inhaling? [1]
  (ii) exhaling? [1]

Exam practice answers and quick quizzes at **www.hoddereducation.co.uk/myrevisionnotes**

(b) Use the scale to work out pulmonary ventilation rate. [1]
(c) What is value of the tidal volume? [1]
(d) Work out the pulmonary ventilation in litres. [1]

2 The diagram shows three model cells. They are cubes of gelatine with dimensions of 1 mm, 2 mm and 3 mm long.

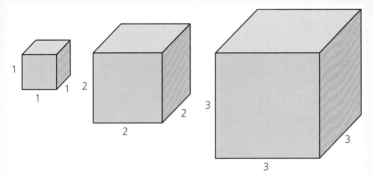

Each model cell was made with gelatine containing a purple indicator that changes to orange in acid conditions. The cubes were placed in weak acid and the time taken for each whole cube to change colour was measured.

(a) The smallest cube weighs 0.002 g. Approximately how much would the largest cube weigh? [1]
(b) Calculate the surface area to volume ratio for the smallest and the largest cubes. [2]
(c) Predict which cube takes the shortest time to change colour when placed in the acid. Explain your answer. [2]
(d) Explain how this investigation illustrates one reason why cells cannot be large. [2]
(e) Evaluate the use of gelatine cubes as model cells. [3]

3 Triglycerides are a major class of lipid. The diagram shows the formation of a triglyceride molecule.

$$H - \overset{\displaystyle H}{\underset{\displaystyle H}{C}} - OH \quad HO - \overset{\displaystyle O}{C} - R_1$$

Glycerol   Fatty acids   →   Triglyceride   + 3H₂O   Water

(a) Give two ways in which the R group of fatty acids can vary. [2]
(b) Name the type of chemical reaction that joins the fatty acids to the glycerol. [1]
(c) Name the bonds that form between the glycerol and the fatty acids. [1]
(d) In total, how many molecules will be formed when the glycerol combines with the fatty acids? Explain your answer. [2]
(e) Describe the difference between a triglyceride and a phospholipid molecule. [2]

4 (a) Explain what is meant by the term *primary structure of a protein*. [2]
(b) The diagram shows cysteine, an amino acid.

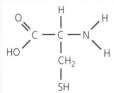

(i) Draw a box around the R group. [1]
(ii) Draw a circle around the amino group. [1]
(c) Disulfide bridges are strong covalent bonds that contribute to structure of a protein. Explain how the amino acid shown can be involved in the maintenance of the tertiary structure. [3]

5 The diagram shows an *E. coli* bacterium, drawn from a micrograph.

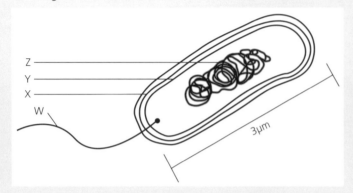

(a) Name the four labelled structures shown. [2]

(b) Name two structures that are normally present in bacterial cytoplasm but are not shown in this diagram. [2]

(c) Suggest why the structures you named in part (b) were not present on the original micrograph. [1]

(d) Use the scale bar to calculate the magnification of the diagram. [2]

(e) This bacterium can swim at a rate of one hundred times its body length per second. Assuming it swims in a straight line, calculate how long it would take the bacterium to cover 1 mm. [2]

6 The table shows the number of deaths due to coronary heart disease per 100 000 population in the UK.

Year	Age 33–44		Age 45–54		Age 55–64		Age 65–74	
	Male	Female	Male	Female	Male	Female	Male	Female
1970	65	11	267	46	727	204	1631	704
1980	56	9	270	50	733	215	1621	688
1990	37	6	159	33	536	179	1352	594
2000	19	5	92	20	291	84	823	347
2008	17	4	67	14	175	47	443	179

Source: British Heart Foundation, Coronary Heart Disease Statistics, 2010

(a) Explain why the figures are given per 100 000 population. [2]

(b) Identify three trends shown by the data. [3]

(c) Identify one risk factor for coronary heart disease and explain how it could account for the change in the data. [2]

Answers and quick quiz 3 online

ONLINE

Summary

By the end of this chapter you should be able to understand:

- How the surface area to volume ratio changes as an organism gets larger.
- The essential features of the gas exchange surfaces of single-celled animals, insects, fish and dicotyledonous plants.
- The basic structure of the human gas exchange system.
- The features of the alveolar epithelium as a surface over which gas exchange occurs.
- How the lungs are adapted for gas exchange.
- Pulmonary ventilation rate as the product of tidal volume and breathing rate.
- The mechanism of breathing.
- The effects of emphysema and asthma on lung function.
- The basic structure of the human heart, including the valves and blood vessels.
- The events of the cardiac cycle, the pressure and volume changes and the associated opening and closing of the valves.
- The electrical events of the cardiac cycle, including the roles of the sinoatrial node (SAN), atrioventricular node (AVN) and bundle of His.
- Cardiac output as the product of stroke volume and heart rate.
- The basics of coronary heart disease, including atheroma as fatty material within the walls of arteries.
- The link between atheroma and the increased risk of aneurysm and thrombosis.
- Myocardial infarction and its cause in terms of an interruption to the blood flow to heart muscle.
- The risk factors associated with coronary heart disease.
- The structure of xylem tissue and the idea of transpiration.
- The cohesion-tension theory as the mechanism that draws water up the xylem.
- The factors affecting transpiration and the use of a potometer.
- The structure of phloem and the mass flow hypothesis for translocation.
- Evidence for the mass flow hypothesis.

4 Genetic information, variation and relationships between organisms

DNA, genes and chromosomes

DNA in prokaryotes and eukaryotes

This section builds on the structure of DNA and RNA covered on pp. 21–23.

The DNA molecules in prokaryotes are short, circular and not associated with organising proteins. In eukaryotes, the DNA is linear and wound around organising proteins called **histones**. This organisation of DNA and its associated proteins forms **chromosomes**, found in all eukaryotic cells (Figure 4.1).

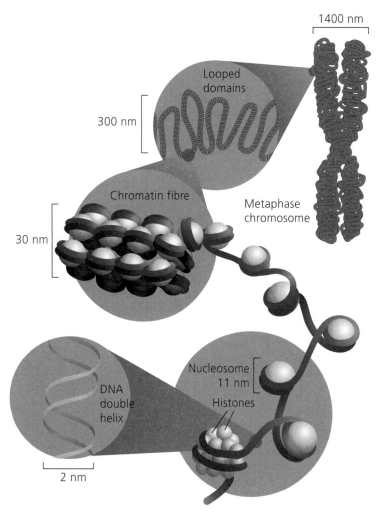

Figure 4.1 After replication, two identical DNA molecules become tightly coiled into a chromosome. Chromatin consists of DNA tightly coiled around organising proteins called histones

Overall, the DNA of **eukaryotes** is found mainly in the nucleus, but there is some in the **mitochondria** and, in plant cells, the **chloroplasts**. The DNA of mitochondria and chloroplasts is circular, which is evidence that these organelles used to be free-living bacteria.

If you look at the nucleus of a non-dividing cell, even with a good microscope, all you can see is, well, mush. In reality, it is a mass of DNA molecules all spread out, so that the genes can be expressed and the DNA can be copied. It is a bit like having the Sunday papers spread out all over the floor. DNA in this state is called **chromatin**. However, when a cell is going to divide it must first copy its DNA and then it must coil it up so it can be equally divided between the new cells. Just like rolling up the newspapers so you can move them around easily.

Each DNA molecule is several centimetres long — an outrageous size for a single molecule. To condense it so that 46 molecules can still fit inside a nucleus requires a lot of organisation — coils within coils within coils. That is what a chromosome is — one long, supercoiled DNA molecule containing hundreds or thousands of genes. The DNA has copied itself exactly, so the chromosomes appear as double structures with two identical sides. Each side, called a **chromatid**, is an exact copy of the other side, joined by a **centromere**.

The total amount of genetic material in an organism is called the **genome**, which includes all the genes and the non-coding sequences in between. Amazingly, the entire genome is present in every body cell. The human genome consists of 23 chromosomes, which occur in pairs. In total, there are over 3 billion base pairs. Different species have different genomes, but it would be wrong to think that the larger the genome, the more complex the organism.

> **Revision activity**
>
> This topic contains a lot of confusing C words. Make a glossary of these words: chromosome, chromatin, centromere, centriole and chromatid.

TESTED ☐

Now test yourself

1 Describe the distribution of DNA in a prokaryotic cell.
2 Describe the distribution of DNA in a eukaryotic cell.

Answer on p. 110

Genes

REVISED ☐

A **gene** is a length of DNA that codes for making a **polypeptide** or a functional **RNA** molecule. A gene is always found at the same position — called a **locus** (plural: loci) — on a chromosome. Different genes have different **base sequences**. A sequence of three DNA bases is known as a **triplet**.

Most genes make proteins. The rule is: one gene makes one polypeptide. Sometimes this polypeptide turns into a functional protein and sometimes it needs to be combined with other polypeptides. Haemoglobin, for example, contains two different polypeptides so it is coded for by two different genes. A relatively small number of genes code for essential RNA molecules such as ribosomal RNA (rRNA) and transfer RNA (tRNA).

Proteins produced by genes are essential for growth, repair and the processes of life. Many of them are enzymes or membrane proteins. Our current best estimate is that the human genome contains about 23 000 genes, although there is much we do not know. We need to know where all the genes are,

> A **gene** is a length of DNA that codes for making one polypeptide or protein. A gene always codes for making a polypeptide, but some proteins consist of more than one polypeptide, in which case it will be coded for by more than one gene.

what they code for, how they combine and, crucially, how they are switched on or off in certain cells at certain times.

Non-coding DNA

In eukaryotes, most of the DNA does not code for polypeptides. If we could stretch out a single eukaryotic DNA molecule and highlight the genes, we would see that they make up less than 10% of the molecule. There are two areas of non-coding DNA:

- Within genes — non-coding sequences within genes are called **introns** whereas coding sequences are called **exons** because they are 'expressed' to make proteins. Introns must be removed by the cells before the protein is made.
- Between genes — there is a lot of non-coding DNA between genes, often consisting of multiple repeats in which the same base sequence is repeated many times. This DNA varies greatly between individuals and its analysis is the basis of DNA profiling.

During transcription, the entire base sequence of a gene is transcribed to produce **pre-mRNA** (Figure 4.2). This includes both the introns and the exons. Before it leaves the nucleus, the pre-mRNA is edited and the introns are removed. The exons are then spliced together to produce **mRNA** that carries only the coding sections of the gene.

> **Messenger RNA (mRNA)** is a nucleic acid that acts as a messenger. It takes a copy of the genetic code from the nucleus into the cytoplasm during protein synthesis. It consists of a single polynucleotide chain with a backbone made of alternating ribose sugars and phosphate groups.

> **Typical mistake**
>
> Candidates sometimes refer to *extrons* when they mean to say *exons*.

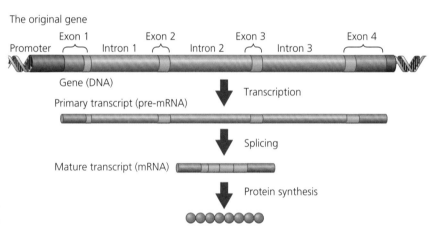

The original gene

Figure 4.2 Following transcription, the introns are spliced out of the mRNA molecule before it can be translated

The genetic code

The **genetic code** is:
- **universal** — the same **codons** code for the same amino acids in all known organisms
- **non-overlapping** — a sequence of CCTGGC is just two codons, CCT and GGC. If the code overlapped there would be codons of CCT, CTG, TGG and GGC. Each base is used once only
- **degenerate** — there are 64 different codons but only 20 amino acids, so there are spare codons. Most amino acids have more than one codon and some, such as leucine, have as many as six (Figure 4.3)

> A **codon** is a sequence of three bases on an mRNA molecule that codes for an amino acid, although there are three codons that do not code for any amino acid. They act as 'stop' signals and indicate the end of a particular protein.

First position	Second position				Third position
	T	C	A	G	
T	Phenylalanine Phenylalanine Leucine Leucine	Serine Serine Serine Serine	Tyrosine Tyrosine (stop) (stop)	Cysteine Cysteine (stop) Tryptophan	T C A G
C	Leucine Leucine Leucine Leucine	Proline Proline Proline Proline	Histidine Histidine Glutamine Glutamine	Arginine Arginine Arginine Arginine	T C A G
A	Isoleucine Isoleucine Isoleucine Methionine	Threonine Threonine Threonine Threonine	Asparagine Asparagine Lysine Lysine	Serine Serine Arginine Arginine	T C A G
G	Valine Valine Valine Valine	Alanine Alanine Alanine Alanine	Aspartic acid Aspartic acid Glutamic acid Glutamic acid	Glycine Glycine Glycine Glycine	T C A G

Figure 4.3 The genetic code

Now test yourself

3 How can you tell that Figure 4.3 contains DNA codes and not RNA codes?
4 Use Figure 4.3 to complete this table.

DNA sequence	AAT		GTC
mRNA sequence		GUA	
Amino acid			

Answer on p. 110

DNA and protein synthesis

The **genome** is the complete set of genes in a cell and the **proteome** is the full range of proteins that the cell is able to produce.

Synthesising a protein

To synthesise a protein, you have to join amino acids in the right order (Figure 4.4). This is exactly what the genetic code does. A protein is a complex molecule that is a long, twisted polymer of amino acids. There are 20 different amino acids that can be joined in any order. These amino acids have names such as valine, leucine, serine and lysine. They are commonly given three-letter abbreviations: val, leu, ser and lys.

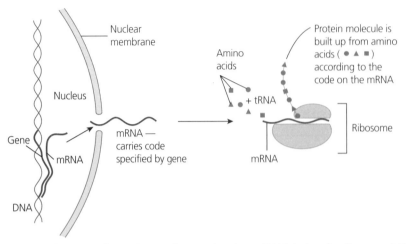

Figure 4.4 An overview of protein synthesis. mRNA is basically a mobile copy of a gene that passes out of the nucleus, taking the genetic code to the ribosome so that the correct protein can be made

Once the amino acids are joined together, many different forces combine to twist and bend the polypeptide chain into a particular shape. The secondary structure refers to structures in part of the molecule, such as helixes and sheets, whereas the tertiary structure is the overall shape of the polypeptide chain.

Now test yourself

TESTED

5 What is the difference between the tertiary and the quaternary structure of a protein?

Answer on p. 110

Complementary bases

REVISED

As there are only four bases but 20 amino acids, the bases are used in sequences of three. A sequence of three bases is known as a triplet, for example CCT or GAA. Each triplet codes for a specific amino acid.

If a protein consists of 100 amino acids, the gene that codes for the protein must have 100 triplets, which is 300 bases. In reality, the gene will be longer because there are usually some non-coding sequences (introns) within the gene as well.

As in DNA replication, the key to protein synthesis is complementary bases (Figure 4.5). When the two strands of DNA are separated, the sequence on the gene can be copied by adding complementary RNA nucleotides. These are similar to DNA nucleotides but the base thymine (T) is replaced by uracil (U). Therefore, if a section of the gene reads TAT GCG TTA, the complementary RNA sequence is AUA CGC AAU.

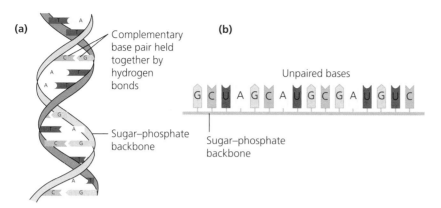

(a)
- Complementary base pair held together by hydrogen bonds
- Sugar–phosphate backbone

(b) Unpaired bases

G C U A G C A U G C G A U G U C

Sugar–phosphate backbone

Exam tip

You don't have to remember any codon or amino acid combinations. These will always be provided in the exam question.

Figure 4.5 The key molecules in protein synthesis. (a) A double-stranded DNA molecule. (b) A single-stranded mRNA molecule

The structure of mRNA and tRNA

REVISED

There are two types of RNA in protein synthesis:
- messenger RNA (mRNA) is a long, single-stranded polynucleotide chain that is assembled on a gene
- transfer RNA (tRNA) is a small clover-leaf shaped 'fetch and carry' molecule that brings amino acids to the site of protein synthesis (Figure 4.6)

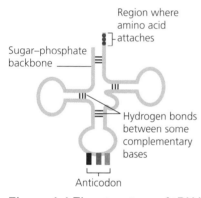

Region where amino acid attaches

Sugar–phosphate backbone

Hydrogen bonds between some complementary bases

Anticodon

Figure 4.6 The structure of tRNA

Table 4.1 Comparing DNA, mRNA and tRNA

Feature	DNA	mRNA	tRNA
Sugar	Deoxyribose	Ribose	Ribose
Bases	A, C, G, T	A, C, G, U	A, C, G, U
Number of strands	Two	One	One
Hydrogen bonds?	Yes	No	Yes
Number of nucleotides	Millions	Hundreds or thousands — it depends on the size of the gene	About 75

Now test yourself

TESTED

6 Give three differences between the structures of mRNA and tRNA.
7 How many different types of tRNA exist in cells? Explain your answer.

Answer on p. 110

In eukaryotes

Transcription is the first stage of protein synthesis. DNA cannot leave the nucleus, but proteins are built on the **ribosomes**. As a consequence, the genetic code must be copied in the nucleus and transferred to the ribosomes. Transcription is the process of copying the genetic code by making mRNA from DNA (Figure 4.7).

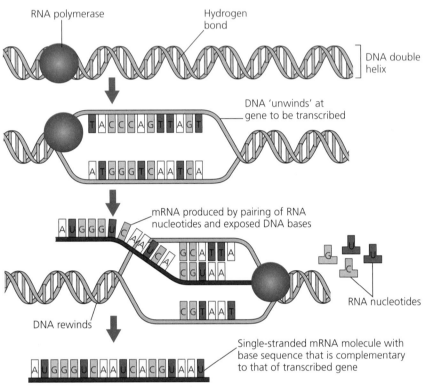

Figure 4.7 Transcription

1 The enzyme **RNA polymerase** attaches to the start of the gene.
2 The DNA unwinds as the hydrogen bonds are broken.
3 The RNA polymerase moves along the gene, catalysing the addition of complementary nucleotides. The entire base sequence is transcribed to produce **pre-mRNA**.
4 Before it leaves the nucleus, the pre-mRNA is edited to form mRNA.
5 The mRNA passes out of the nucleus, through the nuclear pores and into the cytoplasm where it attaches to a ribosome.

In prokaryotes

In bacteria, transcription is slightly different. The mRNA is made on the gene in a similar process to the one for eukaryotes, but there is no splicing out of the introns. The mRNA passes directly to the ribosomes where it is used to make the polypeptide/protein.

Now test yourself

TESTED

8 What is the difference between pre-mRNA and mature mRNA?

Answer on p. 110

> **Typical mistake**
>
> Many candidates state that RNA polymerase adds complementary *bases*, but the correct term is complementary *nucleotides*. It is the bases that actually join, but they also have a sugar and a phosphate attached.

> **Typical mistake**
>
> Many candidates confuse transcription and translation, but make sure you get them the right way round. Remember that *–cription* comes before *–lation* both alphabetically and in biology.

Translation

In eukaryotes

Translation is the second stage of protein synthesis. It involves assembling a protein by joining amino acids together according to the sequence encoded on the mRNA. The key organelle is the ribosome, which can be thought of as a giant enzyme that holds all the different components together so that the process can happen. The tRNA molecules are relatively small, with two key features:

● an anticodon consisting of three bases
● an amino acid binding site

The anticodon and the amino acid are always matched. For example, the mRNA codon AUG codes for the amino acid methionine. When this codon is translated, a tRNA molecule with the anticodon UAC arrives carrying a methionine at the other end.

1 Ribosomes have two codon-binding sites. The first two codons on the mRNA molecule attach to the binding sites.
2 The first codon is translated. It reads AUG, which codes for the amino acid methionine. A tRNA molecule arrives carrying a methionine. The amino acid is held in place (Figure 4.8).
3 The second codon is translated. The second amino acid is brought in by the tRNA molecule and held alongside the first one.
4 An ATP molecule attaches and is hydrolysed. The energy released is used to form the peptide bond between the two amino acids.
5 The mRNA moves alone the ribosome, one codon at a time. The polypeptide grows as each codon is translated (Figure 4.9).

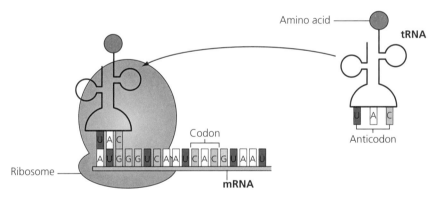

Figure 4.8 Translation, steps 1–2

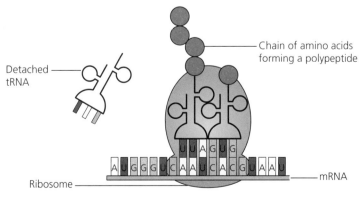

Figure 4.9 Translation, steps 3–5

Revision activity

Draw your own cartoon or storyboard to explain translation — making the components from card works well. You will need a large ribosome, one mRNA with bases, at least two tRNAs with anticodons and an equal number of amino acids.

9 If a polypeptide consists of 62 amino acids, how many nucleotides will the mature mRNA have?
10 Put these events of translation in order.
   A Polypeptide grows
   B mRNA attaches to ribosome
   C Peptide bonds form
   D ATP is split
   E tRNA delivers amino acids and holds them alongside each other
   F The first two codons are translated together
   G mRNA moves along ribosome

Answer on p. 110

Genetic diversity can arise as a result of mutation or during meiosis

A mutation is a change in an organism's genetic material. Mutation can occur at the level of genes or chromosomes.

Gene mutations REVISED

Gene mutations occur because mistakes in **DNA replication** result in a changed **base sequence**. This changes the genotype of the organism and may be inherited. Mutations do not always affect the organism because:

● some take place in the non-coding DNA between genes
● some take place in the introns (non-coding sequences) within genes
● some will still code for the same amino acid — the genetic code is degenerate. For example, if the codon GUU mutates to GUC, GUA or GUG, it will still code for the amino acid valine
● some will cause a change in the amino acid sequence, but this does not significantly change the tertiary structure. The protein is still the right shape and still functions in the organism

Therefore, the only gene mutations that affect organisms are the ones that bring about significant changes in the structure of the protein. There are two main ways in which a base sequence can be altered:

● **base deletion**, in which one base is lost and there is a frame shift — all the bases move along in one direction and therefore many codons are changed
● **base substitution**, in which one base is substituted for another. This is also called a point mutation. Only one codon is changed, but this can still have a significant effect on the protein

In Figure 4.10, the top two rows show the original sequence. The second two rows show the effect of deleting the red letter A: a frame shift results so that all codons and all amino acids are changed. The third two rows show the effect of a substitution. Here, only one codon and one amino acid are changed.

Original base sequence on mRNA	AGA	UAC	GCA	CAC	AUG	CGC
Encoded sequence of amino acids	Arginine	Tyrosine	Alanine	Histidine	Methionine	Arginine
mRNA base sequence after base substitution	AGU	UAC	GCA	CAC	AUG	CGC
Encoded sequence of amino acids	Serine	Tyrosine	Alanine	Histidine	Methionine	Arginine
mRNA base sequence after base deletion	AGU	ACG	CAC	ACA	UGC	GCx
Encoded sequence of amino acids	Serine	Threonine	Histidine	Threonine	Cysteine	Alanine

Figure 4.10 The effects of mutation

Gene mutations occur randomly. The more times DNA is replicated, the greater the chance that there will be a mutation. Most of these mistakes are spotted and corrected by a 'proofreading' mechanism within the cell. The rate of mutation can be increased by **mutagenic agents**, which include:

● some chemicals including benzene, mustard gas and bromine/bromine compounds
● ionising radiation (gamma and X-rays)
● ultraviolet light
● biological agents such as some viruses and bacteria

Chromosome mutations

Chromosome mutations are on a larger scale than gene mutations. If a gene mutation can be likened to changing a word in a sentence, a chromosome mutation can be likened to removing a whole chapter and either throwing it away, inserting it somewhere else, putting it in backwards or attaching it to part of another chapter. As each chromosome contains hundreds or thousands of genes, most chromosome mutations are lethal.

Mutations in the number of chromosomes can arise spontaneously by chromosome **non-disjunction** (meaning 'failure to separate'). During meiosis, each chromosome of a homologous pair should separate and end up in a different **gamete** (Figure 4.11). Non-disjunction results in one gamete getting both chromosomes while the other gets neither.

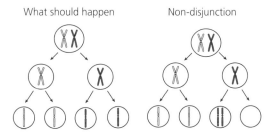

Figure 4.11 Chromosome non-disjunction

Down's syndrome is a common genetic condition caused by non-disjunction of chromosome 21. If it happens in the ovary, one ovum (egg) gets both chromosomes. If this is fertilised by a normal sperm containing one chromosome, the result is three chromosome 21s. If the ovum with no chromosomes 21s is fertilised, the embryo fails to develop. Down's syndrome cannot be described as inherited because it is not passed from parent to child. It is a spontaneous mutation that happens when the gamete is produced. It is a fault of meiosis.

Meiosis

There are two types of cell division:

- **mitosis** — one cell divides once to produce two identical daughter cells (see p. 36)
- **meiosis** — one cell divides twice to produce four **daughter cells**, each of which is genetically different and has half the number of chromosomes of the parent cells

> **Haploid cells** contain one set of chromosomes.
>
> **Diploid cells** contain two sets of chromosomes.

Haploid cells

The only **haploid cells** in humans are the **gametes** (eggs and sperm). They contain 23 chromosomes: one copy of each autosome (22 autosomes) and one sex chromosome (either X or Y). All other cells are **diploid cells**. This means they have two sets of 23 chromosomes each, making a total of 46 chromosomes.

Because our body cells are diploid, this means we have a back-up copy of each gene. If one mutates and does not function, there is another one that does. Diploid cells divide by meiosis to make haploid cells, which fuse to form new, genetically unique individuals.

> **Typical mistake**
>
> Stating that all cells in all organisms have 46 chromosomes — they don't. Human body cells have 46 chromosomes (23 pairs). The cells of most other organisms have a different number of chromosomes.

Homologous chromosomes

There are three golden rules about **homologous chromosomes** (Figure 4.12):

1 They have the same genes.
2 At the same positions (loci).
3 But they may or may not have the same alleles.

> **Homologous chromosomes** are a pair of chromosomes that carry matching genes.

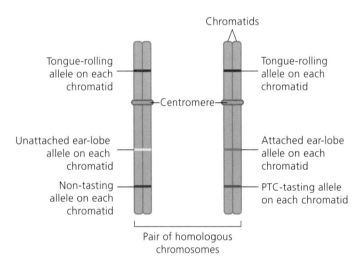

Figure 4.12 A pair of homologous chromosomes with a few genes labelled. Note that the same genes are always at the same loci, but sometimes the alleles are different

> **Exam tip**
>
> Meiosis is a complex process that goes through two divisions. You don't need to know the individual stages, just the ways in which it causes variation. For example, you don't need to know about prophase 1 or metaphase 2.

Genetic recombination

Meiosis creates variation via two processes:

- **Crossing over** (or simply '**crossover**') — homologous chromosomes line up alongside each other and swap blocks of genes. Points of attachment (**chiasmata**) form and sections of chromosome swap between paternal and maternal chromosomes. This process creates new allele combinations.

- **Independent segregation** — at random, one from each of a pair of chromosomes passes into the daughter cell. If there were three pairs of chromosomes, there are 8 (2^3) different combinations of chromosomes that can result.

Once meiosis has created large numbers of unique gametes, a third process guarantees even more variation: **random fertilisation**. Any sperm can fertilise any egg, with the result that every individual is unlike any who has existed before or ever will again.

Now test yourself

11 Human cells have 23 pairs of chromosomes. How many different combinations of chromosome pairs can result from independent segregation in meiosis?

Answer on p. 110

Genetic diversity and adaptation

Genetic diversity can be defined as the number of different **alleles** of **genes** in a population. Without genetic diversity there can be no natural selection and no evolution. If all organisms in a population had the same alleles, they would all be clones, and that is bad.

Natural selection

The idea that species can change over time has been around for centuries, but Charles Darwin was first to come up with a workable mechanism for how the change can actually happen. That mechanism is **natural selection** and, arguably, it is the most important idea in biology. The key points are:
- New alleles are created by **random mutation**.
- Many mutations are harmful but, occasionally, an allele or combination of alleles gives certain individuals an advantage and leads to increased **reproductive success**.
- These individuals pass on their advantageous alleles to the next generation.
- Over many generations there will be a change in the frequency of these new alleles in the population. **Evolution** is defined as a change in allele frequency in a population.

Natural selection results in species that are better adapted to their environment. These adaptations can be:
- **anatomical**, such as a thicker shell
- **physiological**, such as resistance to a particular pesticide
- **behavioural**, such as social cooperation

> **Typical mistake**
>
> In exam questions, candidates often state or imply that organisms evolve in their own lifetime — they don't. It is all about luck. Those that are born lucky, with the right alleles or combinations of alleles, will pass on more of their alleles to the next generation.

> **Typical mistake**
>
> Natural selection is often seen as a matter of life or death, and candidates sometimes state that a poorly adapted individual will die and that stops them reproducing. However, it is often more subtle than that. It is about reproductive success. A better adapted individual reproduces more successfully than a less well adapted one, even though they might live in the same population for years.

Two types of selection

There is a tendency to think that natural selection always leads to evolution, but it can be a force for stability, giving us two basic types of selection: directional and stabilising.

Directional selection

Directional selection (Figure 4.13) is force for change. In this case, extremes of phenotype have an advantage, such as the thickest fur or the deepest roots. A simple example is antibiotic resistance in bacteria. Individuals that possess the resistance allele will survive and so more of the next generation will possess the resistance allele.

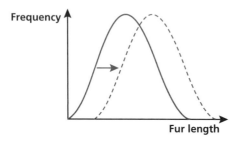

Environmental changes favour the selection of longer fur, causing the normal distribution to shift

Figure 4.13 Directional selection

Stabilising selection

Stabilising selection (Figure 4.14) is seen in cases where the individuals at the extremes of phenotype are at a disadvantage compared with those in the mid-range. Birth weight in humans is a classic example of this. Very large babies cause problems in childbirth whereas very small babies have a lower chance of survival due to a variety of reasons, including a reduced surface area to volume ratio (making them vulnerable to heat loss) and a weakened immune system.

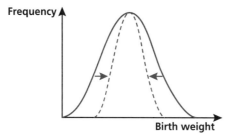

In a stable environment, selection operates to reduce the numbers of heavy and light babies born

Figure 4.14 Stabilising selection

Now test yourself

12 Suggest why stabilising selection tends to reduce diversity.

Answer on p. 110

Species and taxonomy

What is a species? REVISED

A **species** is a group of organisms with observable similarities that can interbreed to produce **fertile offspring**. This definition works well enough for most situations, including A-level exams. It is well known that horses and donkeys can mate to produce sterile hybrids called mules (or asses), and that lions and tigers can produce ligers or tigons, which are also sterile.

However, there are problems with this definition. For example, wolves, coyotes and domestic dogs are all classed as separate species and all have their own scientific names, but they can all interbreed to produce fertile offspring.

Now test yourself TESTED

13 What is the definition of a species?

Answer on p. 110

Courtship behaviour REVISED

In most species of animals, **courtship behaviour** is necessary to ensure **successful mating**. Courtship always involves some type of signal, such as:
- visual — displays, dances, flashes of light
- noises/songs
- pheromones — chemical messengers
- tactile — involving touch

There are several reasons for courtship:
- to find a member of the same species (**species recognition**)
- to approach safely and without aggression — male spiders and praying mantises need to get it right to avoid being eaten, for example
- to choose a strong and healthy mate
- to form a pair bond — many species cooperate over parental care and some mate for life

Not only does courtship allow organisms to find each other, it also helps scientists to identify different species. For example, there are several different species of firefly that look exactly the same, but they have different 'flash' patterns. Finding the right species is important because it avoids infertile matings. If the sperm and egg are not from the same species, they will not be chemically compatible and fertilisation will not take place.

Phylogenetic classification REVISED

The phylogenetic classification system is all about finding out what organisms evolved from what. It is a system of classification based on the evolutionary origins and relationships between organisms and groups of organisms. To construct a phylogenetic tree, scientists use:
- anatomical features, such as body plans
- fossils
- biochemical analysis of base sequences in DNA or amino acid sequences in proteins

Figure 4.15 shows a phylogenetic tree for humans and great apes. For any two species, the golden rule is: the more closely related, the more recently they had a common ancestor. This is the point at which the two species began to evolve along different lines.

Common ancestors are shown by junctions (or nodes) in the diagram. Figure 4.15 shows that the closest relative to humans is the chimpanzee. Gibbons are more distantly related, so humans and gibbons had a common ancestor further back in time.

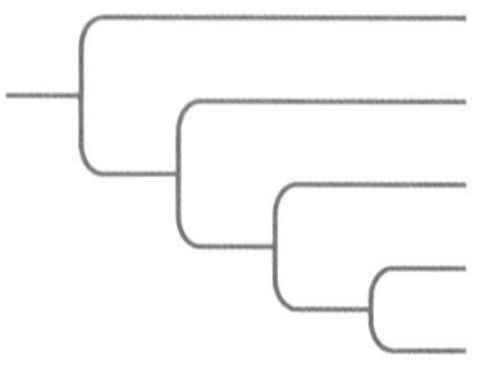

Figure 4.15 The phylogenetic tree for humans and great apes

Now test yourself

TESTED

14 List all the relatives of the gibbon, starting with the closest.

Answer on p. 110

Taxonomy

REVISED

Taxonomy is the science of classification. Scientists are working towards a giant family tree showing the history of life on Earth — what evolved, from what, and when. This will probably never be completed because the extinct species far outnumber the living ones and most of them left no fossils.

Classification is one area of science where there is very little agreement. Systems and ideas are changing constantly as new evidence comes to light. Modern DNA techniques and protein analysis give new evidence about **evolutionary origins** and **relationships**, so that our ideas are changing constantly.

Taxonomic hierarchy

A **hierarchy** is a layered system. The key points of the taxonomic hierarchy are:
- It consists of a series of eight groups, from the most general (domain) to the most specific (species). Similar species are placed in a genus. Similar genera are placed in a family etc. Each group is called a **taxon** (plural: **taxa**).
- The eight groups are **domain**, **kingdom**, **phylum**, **class**, **order**, **family**, **genus** and **species**.
- There is **no overlap** between the groups. For example, there is no organism that is part fish and part amphibian — it is either in one group or the other.
- The groups are based on shared features. The more specific the group, the more shared features there are.

For example, humans and jellyfish are both in the animal kingdom (Table 4.1) because they both share the basic features of animals: they are multicellular, have cells with no walls, move in search of food and digest it in a gut. There, the similarities end.

> **Revision activity**
>
> Think up your own memorable phrase featuring the letters DKPCOFGS to help you remember the groups.

Table 4.1 Classifying humans

Taxon	Humans as an example	Reasons
Domain	Eukaryota	We are organisms whose cells have a distinct nucleus
Kingdom	Animalia	We are animals
Phylum	Chordata	We have a nerve cord — the sub-phylum vertebrata contains animals that have a backbone
Class	Mammal	We have fur and feed our young on milk
Order	Primate	We are social animals with a large brain, opposable thumbs, finger nails, and colour binocular vision
Family	Hominidae	We are man-like apes
Genus	*Homo*	*Homo* means man — there is only one living species in this genus
Species	*sapiens*	'Wise/thinking' man

The binomial system

Currently, there are over 2 million different species that have been discovered and given a scientific name. Many more are yet to be discovered.

Each species is universally identified by its scientific name, which is **binomial** — each name has two parts — the lion is *Panthera leo*, for example — which usually come from Latin or Greek. This name is used across all language barriers and avoids confusion when referring to a particular species.

The first part of the scientific name is the genus, which always has a capital letter. The second part is the specific, or species, name, which is always lower case. When writing scientific names, they should be underlined or in italics.

Now test yourself

15 The binomial name for the cat is *Felis catus*. Which is the genus and which is the species name?

Answer on p. 110

Biodiversity within a community

Biodiversity is a measure of the richness of a habitat or ecosystem. It can apply to a range of **habitats**, regardless of the size or shape of that habitat.

Index of diversity

Biodiversity can be given a numerical value, known as an **index of diversity**, as a result of two measurements:
- the number of species in a **community** (**species richness**)
- the number of individuals of each species (**species evenness**)

Therefore, many individuals from many different species means there is a high diversity. Two classic examples of high-diversity ecosystems are tropical rainforests and coral reefs.

> **Species richness** is the number of different species in a habitat.
>
> **Species evenness** is how evenly each species is represented throughout a habitat.

Now test yourself

16 List two pieces of information needed to calculate an index of diversity.

Answer on p. 110

An index of diversity is a useful measure of the health of an ecosystem. It can also be used to compare one ecosystem with another or to see if anything is changing from year to year. If the index is calculated again at the same time of year and using the same sampling techniques, any difference in value indicates changing conditions. In particular, a lower value would be a worry, suggesting that conditions are deteriorating. Possible causes for change include:

● climate change, such as warmer water causing increased acidity (lower pH)
● overfishing of coral reef fish for food or the aquarium trade
● the introduction of foreign species that out-compete the native species
● pollution

Calculation of an index of diversity

There are several versions of the formula for calculating an index of diversity, so make sure you are consistent. In this case, we will use the formula:

$$d = \frac{N(N-1)}{\Sigma n(n-1)}$$

where:

N = the total number of individuals in all species

n = the total number of individuals in a particular species

Example

Look at the numbers of fish from a coral reef in Table 4.2.

Table 4.2 **Data on fish numbers in a coral reef**

Species	Number of individuals
Clown fish	16
Butterfly fish	9
Four-spot butterfly fish	5
Queen angelfish	2
Koran angelfish	1
Clown triggerfish	2

If an exam question asks you to work out an index of diversity, one approach is to add extra columns to carry out further calculations (Table 4.3).

Table 4.3 **Calculating an index of diversity**

Species	Number of individuals (*n*)	*n* – 1	*n* (*n* – 1)
Clown fish	16	15	240
Butterfly fish	9	8	72
Four-spot butterfly fish	5	4	20
Queen angelfish	2	1	2
Koran angelfish	1	0	0
Clown triggerfish	2	1	2
Total	**35**		**Σ = 336**

Substituting the values into the formula:

$$d = \frac{N(N-1)}{\Sigma\, n\,(n-1)}$$

$$= \frac{35 \times 34}{336}$$

$$= \frac{1190}{336}$$

$$= 3.54$$

Therefore, the index of diversity in this example is 3.54.

The effects of farming on biodiversity

REVISED

Farming techniques can reduce biodiversity. In the UK, for example, farming involves the increasing use of technology. Agricultural practices that can affect biodiversity include:

● **Deforestation** — although most deforestation took place in the UK centuries ago, it is a massive worldwide problem. Removal of trees obviously reduces tree diversity as well as removing vital niches for a wide variety of other species.
● **Monoculture** — supermarkets want to buy from just a few large suppliers rather than lots of small ones. It makes economic sense to have large fields growing just one crop, such as wheat or potatoes, which can be harvested efficiently using large machines.
● **Removal of hedgerows** — this turns small fields into large ones, providing more space for crops and making it easier to use large machines. Hedgerows are important habitats for many native species. It used to be a widespread belief that hedgerows also harboured pests and competed with the crops for nutrients, but recent research shows that hedges actually help crops and are just as likely to contain species that eat pests.
● **Use of pesticides** — herbicides kill weeds that compete with the crop for light and nutrients whereas insecticides kill insect pests. It is difficult to make and apply a pesticide that will kill only the pest and nothing else.

Now test yourself

17 List four human activities that reduce biodiversity.
18 Give two reasons why deforestation reduces biodiversity.
19 Explain how the eradication of weeds leads to a reduction in animal diversity.

Answer on p. 110

Investigating diversity

Modern technology allows us to study the DNA and proteins in organisms, which is much more precise than studying body plans or fossils. Advanced sequencing techniques allow us to see how closely related two species are by comparing the base sequences in the DNA or the amino acid sequences in proteins. The basic idea is simple: the more sequence differences there are, the more distantly related the species.

Mutations and changes to the DNA base sequence

The sequence differences come from the process of mutation. The more distantly related the two species, the more time that has elapsed since they had a common ancestor and the more opportunities there have been for mutations to occur.

Mutations change the DNA base sequence. Sometimes, changes in the base sequence also lead to a change in the amino acid sequence, but not all mutations change amino acid sequences because:
● most DNA occurs in between genes — it is non-coding DNA
● there is some non-coding DNA within genes in sections called introns
● sometimes a changed base sequence still codes for the same amino acid — some amino acids can have as many as six different triplet codes

Vitally, the mutations that do change amino acid sequences must be subtle. The changes must be minor otherwise the tertiary structure would be changed and the protein would not work. A non-functional protein is usually a major disadvantage and so the mutation dies with the organism. Therefore, only these very minor changes to proteins accumulate over time.

In order to compare proteins, you should study one that all organisms have, such as **cytochrome C**, which is found in the inner mitochondrial membrane and has a vital role in respiration. As a consequence, it can be used to compare virtually all eukaryote species.

Genetic diversity

It is important to be able to measure **genetic diversity** within a species. A species with very little variation will struggle to adapt to any kind of environmental change. It is also important to be able to measure the genetic differences between different species. This gives us the basic information we require in order to construct evolutionary trees that show us what evolved from what.

There are several ways of measuring this genetic diversity:

1 **frequency of measurable or observable characteristics** — for example, spots on ladybirds or bands on snail shells
2 **base sequence of DNA** — different alleles have different base sequences
3 **base sequence of mRNA** — if there are different alleles, they will code for different mRNAs
4 **amino acid sequence** of the proteins encoded by DNA and mRNA

With **gene technology** (methods 2, 3 and 4), remember that the more the sequences are different, the more distantly related the organisms. This is because mutations accumulate over time.

Standard deviation and investigating variation within a species

When investigating variation, it is not normally possible to look at every individual in a population. So, we have to look at a **sample**. We cannot get a realistic idea of the range of normal values unless we collect **random samples**, which means data collected without **bias**, i.e. without the conscious choice of the experimenter.

When taking measurements, we want to get an understanding of what constitutes a normal range of values without our ideas being distorted by extreme individuals. **Standard deviation** expresses the spread of the data that is one-third either side of the **mean value** (Figure 4.16). One-third is 33.3%, which is normally rounded up to 34%, giving us a measure of the spread of the middle 68% of values.

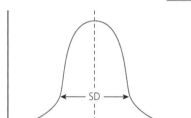

Figure 4.16 Standard deviation

For example, when measuring adult male height we could say that the standard deviation is 1.75 m ± 0.05, meaning that the mean height of adult males in our sample is 1.75 m and that 68% of them are between 1.7 m and 1.8 m tall.

> **Exam tip**
>
> Don't refer to *average* when you are referring to the *mean*. This is because median and mode are also types of average.

> **Exam tip**
>
> The AS specification clearly states that candidates will not be required to calculate standard deviations, but you might be asked to calculate the mean of a set of values.

Now test yourself

20 Explain why standard deviation is not calculated using all of the measurements in a sample.

Answer on p. 110

Exam practice

1 If two organisms belong to the same family, to which other taxonomic groups do they also belong? [1]

2 These data were obtained from DNA hybridisation studies on great apes.

Species involved	Temperature at which hybrid DNA denatured (°C)
Human/human	94.0
Human/orangutan	90.4
Human/chimpanzee	92.4
Human/gorilla	91.7

(a) Explain why human/human DNA denatures at the highest temperature. [3]

(b) (i) Which species is the most distantly related to humans? [1]

   (ii) Explain your answer to part (i). [2]

3 Cytochrome C is a commonly studied protein. It consists of 104 amino acids and is located in the mitochondria, where is has a vital function in respiration. The table shows the differences in the amino acid sequence between human cytochrome C and various other species.

Species pairings	Number of differences
Human/chimpanzee	0
Human/fruit fly	29
Human/horse	12
Human/rattlesnake	14
Human/rhesus monkey	1
Human/screw-worm fly	27
Human/snapping turtle	15
Human/tuna	21

(a) Why is cytochrome C a good protein to use in this type of study? [1]

(b) What is the minimum number of bases that must be contained in the gene for cytochrome C? [1]

(c) Explain why the actual number of bases is likely to be higher. [1]

(d) (i) Suggest which animal is the most distantly related animal to humans. [1]

   (ii) Explain your answer to part (i). [3]

(e) Evaluate the statement: 'Humans are more distantly related to snapping turtles than to rattlesnakes.' [2]

4 A scientist studied the diversity of two areas of forest. The numbers of individuals of all species in the two habitats are given in the table below.

| Species | Number of individuals in: | |
	Habitat A	Habitat B
A	34	87
B	30	2
C	25	1
D	30	1
E	15	1
F	0	1
G	0	1

(a) Explain what is meant by the term *random* sampling. [1]

(b) Which habitat shows the greatest species evenness? Explain your answer. [1]

(c) Use the following formula to calculate the diversity index of habitat B. [2]

$$d = \frac{N(N-1)}{\Sigma n(n-1)}$$

(d) Suggest three human activities that could result in a lowering of the index of diversity. [3]

5 Complete the table with a tick if each statement is correct or a cross if it is false. [3]

	Mitosis	Meiosis
DNA replicates		
Chromosome number is maintained		
Homologous chromosomes pair up		

6 The diagram shows the chromosomes in an organism where $2n = 6$.

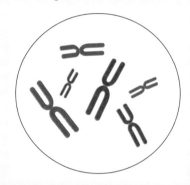

(a) Draw the chromosomes as they would appear after the first meiotic division. [2]

(b) Draw the chromosomes as they would appear after the second meiotic division. [2]

Answers and quick quiz 4 online

ONLINE

Summary

By the end of this chapter you should be able to understand:

- The distribution of DNA in prokaryotic and eukaryotic cells.
- The genetic code as a series of triplets.
- The distribution of coding and non-coding DNA in a cell.
- The processes of transcription and translation, including the roles of the different types of RNA.
- The ways in which meiosis can produce variation.
- The mechanism of natural selection and the two basic types of selection.
- The definition of a species in terms of observable similarities and the ability to produce fertile offspring.
- Courtship behaviour and how it can be used to distinguish different species.

- Phylogenetic groups are based on patterns of evolutionary history.
- Classification systems consist of a hierarchy in which groups are contained within larger composite groups and there is no overlap.
- One hierarchy comprises domain, kingdom, phylum, class, order, family, genus and species.
- Each species is universally identified by a binomial name.
- Biodiversity can be measured by an index of diversity that involves the number of different species and the number of individuals of each species.
- Farming techniques can reduce biodiversity.
- Evolutionary differences can be assessed by looking at base sequences in DNA and amino acid sequences in proteins.
- Standard deviation is a measure of the spread of the data about the mean.

Now test yourself answers

Chapter 1

1 Condensation

2 Hydrolysis

3 Consists of long, straight, unbranched chains of β-glucose; which lie parallel; and form H bonds along their whole length; forming fibres of great strength.

4 Qualitative tests tell you *what* is present whereas quantitative tests tell you *how much* is present. (Think: quantity = amount)

5 Add ethanol to a sample of cake, shake and then pour off the liquid into water. If the sample contains lipid, a white emulsion is formed.

6 (a) C, H, O

(b) C, H, O

(c) C, H, O, N

7 Proteins, starch and glycogen

8 Enzymes provide an alternative reaction pathway; lower the activation energy; make it easier to achieve the transition state.

9 The transition state is the point at the top of the curve. Once reached, the reaction will go on to completion.

10 Enzymes have an active site that is complementary to the substrate in terms of shape and chemical charges. Different substrates are not complementary.

11 The lock and key model is when the substrate fits exactly into the active site. The induced-fit model is when the active site modifies or changes shape to fit around the substrate.

12 The tertiary structure changes because the weak bonds that maintain it are disrupted/changed/broken.

13 TTGATCCAT

14 Original strand of DNA, nucleotides, DNA helicase, DNA polymerase

15 Hydrogen bonds

16 The nucleus

17 When DNA replicates, in each new DNA molecule one strand is original and one is new.

Chapter 2

1 The roots do not receive light and so they cannot photosynthesise.

2 (a) Eukaryotic

(b) Prokaryotic

(c) Eukaryotic

(d) Prokaryotic

3

	TEM	SEM
Image	2D	3D
Colour	Usually black and white	Can be coloured
Thickness of sample	Must be a thin section	Can be a solid specimen
Resolution	Higher	Lower

4 Four different nucleotides (sugar–phosphate plus A, T, C or G).

5 By facilitated diffusion. (It is water soluble, so it cannot pass through the phospholipids. Therefore, it has to pass through a specific protein channel, which by definition is facilitated diffusion.)

6 Molecules have more kinetic energy, so they bounce around, collide and spread more quickly.

7 Water will pass to the cell with the water potential of $-250\,kPa$ because it always passes to the area with the lowest water potential.

8 Plant cells have a cell wall that prevents them swelling and bursting.

9 (a) 50 (because it only goes to equilibrium)

(b) All 100

10 (a) Respiration

(b) Mitochondria

11 A process in which two substances are absorbed together, such as sodium and glucose.

12 Any four from: skin, mucous membranes, stomach acid, blood clotting, lysozyme in tears and sweat, ear wax, low vaginal pH.

13 No. Glucose is present in all cells, so it cannot be used to identify cells as 'foreign'.

14 Antigens are molecules that are not normally found in the body of the host and they stimulate the production of complimentary antibodies. Pathogens and other foreign cells are covered in antigens. Antibodies are proteins produced by B lymphocytes in response to a particular antigen.

15 Antibodies are proteins, and as such are too large and complex to be made in the lab.

16 Breast milk contains antibodies whereas formula milk does not.

17 A type of lymphocyte that lasts for many years and, on exposure to the antigen, can launch a rapid immune response. Memory cells rapidly divide into a clone of plasma calls that can quickly make antibodies.

18 The primary immune response results from first exposure to an antigen. The secondary immune response results from the second exposure to the same antigen. The secondary immune response produces antibodies more quickly, in greater amounts and for longer than the primary immune response.

19 If people are not vaccinated, the percentage of the population that is vaccinated may be too low to prevent the chain of transmission. Therefore, the herd effect may not be effective.

Chapter 3

1 Volume of oxygen used per gram per unit time, for example $cm^3 g^{-1} min^{-1}$.

2 They have a large surface area to volume ratio and can exchange gas over their whole body surface. The diffusion pathways are very small.

3 To ventilate: to pump fresh air into its tracheal system, so as to maintain a diffusion gradient.

4 It is a countercurrent system. It maintains a diffusion gradient along the whole length of the lamellae.

5 An equilibrium would be reached. Half of the available oxygen would be lost.

6 Respiration is the chemical process that releases the energy from organic molecules. Breathing is ventilation: the act of forcing fresh air (or water) over the gas exchange surfaces. (All cells in all organisms respire, but not all organisms breathe.)

7 Many alveoli provide a large surface area. Thin alveolar cells (squamous epithelium) provide a short diffusion pathway. An efficient blood flow and ventilation maintains the diffusion gradient.

8 Gas exchange is slower/less efficient because the alveolar walls have less surface area and are thicker. Activity requires more oxygen for muscular contraction.

9 Condensation reactions involve smaller molecules joining to make larger ones; water is produced. Hydrolysis reactions involve splitting larger molecules to form smaller ones; water is used.

10 In the cell-surface membranes of the gut epithelial cells (they are in the microvilli).

11 The small intestine (ileum).

12 They are not lost in the faeces. They keep on being re-used without having to be re-synthesised, which would be a waste of energy and resources.

13 Bile salts emulsify lipids, making smaller droplets that have a larger surface area for the lipase enzymes to work on and speeding up digestion.

14 The absorbed substances lower the water potential of the blood, so water flows into the blood by osmosis (water follows the solute).

15 There is more room for haemoglobin, so the cells can carry more oxygen.

16 To speed up the delivery of oxygen. (The enzyme speeds up the reaction between carbon dioxide and water, and in turn the resulting acid lowers the affinity of haemoglobin for oxygen.)

17 The affinity of haemoglobin for oxygen varies according to the conditions. The affinity is high in the lungs and lower in the respiring tissues.

18 (a) Coronary artery
   (b) Pulmonary artery
   (c) Renal artery

19 The cells are thin and permeable, providing a short diffusion pathway and maximising the efficient exchange between tissue fluid and blood.

20 Any three from: oxygen; glucose; amino acids; fatty acids; water; various ions such as sodium, chloride and potassium; vitamins.

21 D, C, B, A

22 No. The atrioventricular valves must shut in order for ventricular pressure to build. If the pressure does not build, the semilunar valves will not open.

23 The atria

24 Left ventricle

25 (a) B and C
   (b) It would show the same pattern, but at lower pressure.

26 The stimulus for the heart beat is generated by the heart muscle itself. (If you cut the nerves to the heart, is keeps on beating.)

27 To allow the ventricles to fill with blood before they contract.

28 cardiac output = stroke volume × heart rate

$$= 100 \times 160$$

$$= 16\,000\,cm^3,\ or\ 16\ litres$$

29 Yes. Someone with a BMI of over 30 is classed as obese.

$$BMI = \frac{mass\ (kg)}{height^2\ (m^2)}$$

$$= \frac{94}{1.56^2}$$

$$= 38.6$$

30 Transpiration is the loss of water vapour (by evaporation) from the upper surfaces of a plant. The transpiration stream is the movement of water and minerals through the plant in the xylem tissue.

31 Translocation is the movement of organic molecules (mainly sucrose) around the plant form source to sink in the phloem fibres. Transpiration is the loss of water vapour (by evaporation) from the upper surfaces of a plant.

Chapter 4

1 In a prokaryotic cell, the DNA is circular. There is one main chromosome and many smaller loops called plasmids.

2 In a eukaryotic cell, the DNA is linear. Most of the DNA is enclosed in the nucleus. There is some (circular) DNA in the mitochondria.

3 They contain uracil (U) and not thymine (T).

4

DNA sequence	AAT	**CAT**	GTC
mRNA sequence	**UUA**	GUA	**CAG**
Amino acid sequence	**Asn**	**His**	**Val**

5 The tertiary structure is the overall 3D shape of the polypeptide. The quaternary structure is the overall shape of proteins that contain more than one polypeptide.

6 mRNA is variable in length, not folded and contains no hydrogen bonds. tRNA is fixed length, folded and has H bonds.

7 There are 64 types because there are 64 different anticodons.

8 Pre-mRNA contains introns. Mature RNA has had the introns removed (spliced out).

9 $62 \times 3 = 186$

10 B, F, E, D, C, G, A

11 $2^{23} = 8\,388\,608$

12 It tends to select for similar individuals with similar genotypes.

13 A group of organisms with observable similarities that can interbreed to produce fertile offspring.

14 Orangutan, gorilla, chimpanzee, human

15 Genus = *Felis*, species = *catus*

16 The number of species present and the number of individuals of each species.

17 Any four from: deforestation, monoculture, removal of hedgerows, use of pesticides, use of fertilisers, other examples of habitat destruction (e.g. construction works).

18 There are fewer tree species and fewer niches for other organisms.

19 Weeds provide niches for insects and other invertebrates, which in turn support the food chain.

20 To avoid the mean being distorted by extreme individual readings.